BRITAIN WENT TO WAR for Pola
Montgomery had effectively to apologise to General Sikorski that
he had no clear idea even where the country was, let alone what
its history had been. Poland has one of strangest and most exotic
cultures, the bravest and most tragic of recent histories, of all
European nations. It suffered all the major traumas of the 20th
century in the most direct form: invasions by Russia and
Germany resulting in the almost unimaginable loss of one in five
of its population; the last pogrom in the world happened in 1946
in Kielce; then the imposition of Communism and the long fight
against it, during which 10 million Poles fought for Solidarity
and helped precipitate the 1989 revolutions, with their painful
aftermath of a brutal transition towards capitalism.

A group of British writers – among them some very
distinguished names – watched these changes at close hand, most
of them having lived in Poland for three or four years, and a number of them having married Polish partners. Yet, apart from
fictional representations, or pseudonymous articles in e.g. *The
New Statesman*, the convention of their employment made it hard
for the story to be told until recently, when Foreign Office rules
were changed. These are the lecturers in English literature
associated with the British Council from 1938 onwards. Some
helped in the reopening of departments of literature after their
closure under Stalin (1947-58); some experienced the imposition
of martial law, during which one Marxist lecturer, on seeing the
tanks come out, fled the country. Many witnessed the birth-pangs
of the new capitalism. As the posts no longer exist, this book is in
part a commemoration of a unique period and programme in
Anglo-Polish cultural relations.

Cold War,
Common Pursuit

*British Council lecturers
in Poland, 1938-1998*

edited by
Peter J. Conradi & Stoddard Martin

Starhaven

Editorial arrangement
© Stoddard Martin 1999
ISBN 0-936315-11-3

Starhaven
Box 2573, La Jolla, CA 92038, USA
in UK, ℅ 42 Frognal, London NW3 6AG

Designed and set in Excelsior by John Mallinson.
Printed on vellum paper and bound by
CPI Copyspeed, 38 Ballard's Lane, London N3 2BJ.

Contents

Alastair Niven

Foreword

My mother had a soft spot for Polish soldiers. In the War years she would frequently travel by train between London and Edinburgh with three young boys in tow, the youngest a future Director of Literature at the British Council. 'It was always the Poles who offered one a seat,' she would say. So I grew up with this knowledge of Polish courtesy and charm. It was confirmed when, as a visiting speaker engaged by the British Council rather than as one its employees, which I am now, I first set foot in Poland in 1986. James Berry, the Jamaican poet based in Britain, and I were taking part in a teachers' seminar in Poznań. We chose our week well. One day, after strolling round a lake in a fine drizzle, we learned of the ghastly radioactive spill at Chernobyl. The cloud carrying the fallout had passed above as we walked, or so we believed at the time, though subsequent doubt has been cast upon this. 'If you ever get cancer,' my doctor confided in me on my return to England, 'you won't know if this caused it or not, so just forget it'. 'It looks as if Poland,' he added, 'may really have got into your blood!'

This collection of essays, which I have been asked to introduce, is full of mordant or droll touches of humour that put me in mind of my laconic doctor. Life was often bleak for the inhabitants of this book, but they rarely, Britons and Poles alike, lost their ability to smile. I suspect they came closest to it when they heard that the British Council would be winding up its lectureship scheme which, over forty years, had brought to Poland a company of teachers of extraordinary talent and humanity. The last lecturer completed his Council contract in 1998. This volume memorialises the contribution of these men and women to Polish life – implicitly to British life too – and there is a melancholy undertow of regret that the scheme has been allowed to wither. In the Afterword by Emma Harris, a figure who has 'straddled the Polish-British divide' for much of the period covered, the regret becomes overt.

However much we may sympathise with these sentiments, there is little point in the Council being defensive about a decision it took openly, consciously and for many reasons. The modern Council is as subject to financial constraints and to new modes of management as any publicly funded organisation in any part of the world. Academic methods have altered too. Thanks to some of the changes charted in this book, particularly those of the last ten years, Poles now have more opportunities to travel and to learn English abroad. Walking down the streets of Warsaw and Łódź, as I did recently, one sees how this once strange and very different world is now superficially much the same as London or Sheffield: hamburger bars, international brand names in the shop windows, sex clubs, western newspapers in the kiosks. It would be surprising if the Council's education policy had stood still when all around it had changed. No one denies that something precious was lost with the discontinuation of the lecturer posts, but would there not in the 21st century be a whiff of neo-colonial patronage about it if the scheme were still to be in place?

The point of this book is not to throw light of any kind – a harsh spotlight or a tender glow – upon the present arrangements whereby the Council promotes literature in Poland, but rather to record a wonderful story, or set of stories, before the memories go[1]. I have worked in universities myself, been an administrator in several official bodies, directed a charitable institution and served on innumerable committees. Almost without exception they do not know their own history. The Council took steps to avoid this on the occasion of its fiftieth anniversary by commissioning the late Frances Donaldson to write a book recording its own past[2]. Alas, when I joined the Council two years ago, I encountered a new generation of Council staff who were unaware that this admirable publication existed. Anything that can be done to remind people that they live in a continuum of moments, and not just in one, must be a good thing. Hence my

Alastair Niven

conviction that *Cold War, Common Pursuit* is a volume which the Council needs for itself as much as for the Polish and British general readers who will, I hope, be encountering it.

They will find an enthralling collection of essays here. I frankly feared, when I first heard of the proposal to publish a book of reminiscences by Council lecturers in English who had worked in Poland, that the writing would alternate between nostalgia and rant, that authors would be driven by an ideological sympathy or antipathy to Communism, and that it might be terribly dull. Instead I find in essay after essay elegant, humane, versatile and captivating evocations of urbscapes, seasons, friendships and academic programmes. Only with the last of these could I – echoing a point persuasively made by Professor Harris – wish for a little more. The people telling their stories here were teachers, but we are given fewer insights into what they taught and how they taught it than I would like.

What we do have are several versions of an unfurling love of Poland in the people who write these essays. No one leaves the country wishing they had never set foot there or desiring not to return. Denis Hills and Witold Ostrowski, the latter providing us with an essential insight into how the Poles regarded the British lecturers among them, have the longest memories. Hills, who was in Poland before the British Council formally took up a role there, gives us vignettes of Jewish communities in the 1930s. Indeed, despite its title this is not a book only about the period of the Cold War: there are pre-, post- and anti-war recollections here. The Communist authorities lurk in the background of most of the pieces, however. More often they are obstacles to be avoided or irritants to be ignored. British stiff upper lip characterises even the more radical and un-Buchanesque contributors. The late Frank Tuohy, for example, remembers that 'My room was searched fairly frequently; I don't smoke, and fag ends would be left in the ashtrays. When I found the searchers *in flagrante*, I complained but I can't say I seriously minded.'

Everyone assumed that there was in any company they kept someone who was what Tuohy calls 'our link with Authority' Even I recall that. When we did a round of introductions at our British Council seminar in Poznań in 1986 one of the people present said to us, 'You ought to know that one of our number will be reporting back to Them everything that goes on here. We don't know which of us it is, but we just ignore them. You should do the same.' These were bold words, more easily uttered in the mid-1980s with Solidarity in the background, albeit illegally, than they were in the 1950s and '60s, but they were unspoken and yet understood throughout the main part of the period this book covers. 'I shall never know if any of my students or colleagues were "spying" on me,' writes Jessica Munns, more cautiously. 'Occasionally, someone would take me aside and inform me that this or that faculty member or student was a "spy", but it was never clear if this confidence was passing malice, a moment of sensationalism or the truth.' Stephen Romer graphically describes how the authorities were dodged and outwitted.

Life was physically hard for the lecturers and harder still for those they taught. Derwent May locates this partly in the combination of harsh weather and grim industrialisation, at least in Łódź where he was based. Michael Irwin comments on the 'thickets of stultifying bureaucracy'. George Hyde has a more fantastical explanation. 'Poland already seemed to me the most semiotic, metaphoric, transformation-scene of a society I had ever encountered outside of the pages of *Alice in Wonderland*.' Perhaps this is why moral positions were often veiled and tentative. 'People knew what they disbelieved but not what they did believe,' says Irwin.

There is a record of beliefs in these essays, however. Roman Catholicism was pervasive. Not every Communist was a time-serving hypocrite. British Council officials upheld honourable standards, though at times in these chapters they are gently mocked for doing so. Even their loo paper, says Munns, made one feel 'abused and privileged to use it': the perfect public school mixture. Above all, there were the lecturers themselves, utterly committed to a belief in the value of art and literature, the integrity of human potential and the efficacy of language well used. The title of this book, with its emphasis on 'common pursuit,' may suggest that they were all Leavisites, but this was the case with only some of them.

By the time we reach the end of the 1970s, as described by Gary Mead, there is a mood of decadence in Poland. The socialist

Alastair Niven

ideal had largely collapsed into self-interest. People were sucked into Intelligence, or thought to be so. Everyone was suspicious of everyone else, Mead infers. Yet the life of the Council and its lecturers went on much as before, all part of a *comédie* sometimes *noire* but more often *humaine*. Both Poles and 'Brits' became increasingly unconvinced by any kind of dogma. As Sean Molloy's diary entry for 27 May 1984 says, 'I tell them it is possible to dislike both Thatcherism and Polish Communism.' The new Polish Pope alone inspired trust in the possibility of unwavering conviction.

And so to the 1990s, a new era of freedom and change, of some losses as well as many precious gains. This volume is for me like overhearing voices in lamplight. It brings me tantalisingly close to a period in Polish history which should not be forgotten and to the life of the British Council within it. I am proud to belong now to an organisation which brought people of the calibre of the authors in this book into the lives of Polish students and teachers. The Council performed well in these years, even if some of its officials look, as they are recalled out of time, slightly comic. Won't we all seem like that to those who come after us? I am proud, too, to work for an organisation that wants to know its own history and is even prepared to put a little money towards reconstructing it, as the Council in both Warsaw and London has done by providing modest help towards this publication.

Peter Conradi had the idea for the book. Encouraged by the Council's Director of Literature at the time, Harriet Harvey Wood, he commissioned the original core of essays. Stoddard Martin has carried the project through to publication. We should be grateful to them, and to all the authors of these essays. Poland is 'a little patch of ground' in *Hamlet*. The makers of *Cold War, Common Pursuit* make it seem like the world's fulcrum, and why not?

---

[1] What the Council offers in place of the lectureship scheme is a full time Literature Officer, based in Warsaw and charged with working in partnership with Polish institutions of higher education to present programmes appropriate to local needs and responsive to the diversity of

modern literary culture. He works in close co-operation with the Council's
Literature Department in London. The person appointed to this post at
present is Cathal McCabe, who speaks fluent Polish and who forms a
natural bridge between the old system, in which he himself was a lecturer,
and the new. As his contribution to this book shows he is a talented poet as
well.

[2] *The British Council: The First Fifty Years*, Jonathan Cape, 1984.

Denis Hills

Warsaw Pre-War

Herr Mark was headmaster of the village school in Eggers-dorf, an old Protestant settlement surrounded by pine woods twenty miles east of Berlin, and it was he who gave me – a young Oxford undergraduate – my first insight into the passionate hostility generated by central European politics. In the summer of 1933 he used to give me German lessons in his sandy vegetable garden among the hollyhocks and rhubarb. When the afternoon train to Warsaw thundered past, he would open his school atlas at the map of what used to be West Prussia and had now, since the Treaty of Versailles, reverted to Poland, and point to the town of Gnesen (Gniezno). 'My birth place', he said. 'When the Poles took over at the end of the war I was driven out with my family. Mark my words, Mr Denis. The day will come when we Germans will reconquer with the sword our lost homelands.'

Two years later I had my first glimpse of Poland. I had just spent three months travelling rough, with knapsack and raincoat, among the German-speaking minorities who lived in thick clusters outside the frontiers of the Reich. Starting in the South Tirol – where Mussolini's soldiers were fortifying the Brenner Pass with gun emplacements – I had ended up on the Baltic, thence returning to Berlin via Danzig Free State and the Polish Corridor. As I was about to board the Berlin train at the frontier station of Piła, and took my last look at the Polish countryside – the rutted cobblestones, farm carts and flowers, the bright head-cloths of women and the wayside crucifixes – I felt an irresistible desire to come back to this mysterious Slavonic world beyond the Oder with its incomprehensible language and dramatic history of servitude and independence. I had had enough of

Germans, of their thumping jackboots and hooked crosses, the outstretched arms and roar of voices at Nazi rallies. During the last three years I had seen the Germans change under Hitler from a people still smarting from poverty and defeat into brown-shirted bullies. When I stopped at Eggersdorf to say goodbye to Herr Mark and his family the eldest son took me aside and told me that the next war would start with a German attack on Poland – 'the only country with enough spirit to stand up to Hitler'. So the bully would attack the underdog, and a 'cause' was at stake: one that had a strongly emotional appeal to any young Oxford graduate.

My opportunity to revisit Poland came at the end of 1936. I spotted an advertisement in *The Times* for an assistant editor of a Polish cultural magazine published in English by the Baltic Institute of Gdynia, applied and was accepted for the post, and sailed from Hays Wharf to Gdynia in the Polish cargo ship *Lech*. The Institute had its offices on the sea-front. I was told never to open the window, handed a pile of manuscripts by Dr Borowik, the Director, and left to get on with them. It was a bitterly cold winter; with lodgings on a small hill above the town I used to sprint to work to keep warm. Gdnyia was a brand-new port sited on an old Kashubian fishing village. It had been heavily sub-sidised by French capital and was still under construction. Unfinished roads and housing blocks petered out in building plots and wooden scaffolding. Many workers lived in shanties. On their way to work on an icy morning they would gulp down small bottles of vodka (małpki) and litter the gutter with empties. Brash, new and entirely dependent on its import and export trade, Gdynia had little cultural life. There was no theatre, only one decent night-club (Maskot), and the honky-tonks in the harbour area were given over to roaming Lascars and Swedish seamen. The small British community, however, had an Anglo-Polish Society which invited guest speakers. These included Ruttledge, the Everest climber, and Robert Byron who described his travels in Persia – he was sallow and flabby and didn't look at all like a 'real' explorer. In those days summer tourists went to Sopot, which had a casino (Müller's) – its walls were papered with old German inflationary banknotes – and to Orlowa where they could bathe from the sand dunes. Gdynia, as

Poland's maritime base, had a naval cadet school and a handsome training yacht, *Dar Pomorza*. During its short career Gdynia had attracted a special sort of adventurer and sharp business man. 'It's like the Klondyke,' a Polish colleague told me, 'full of rogues, bankrupts and divorcees.' Nevertheless the Poles could be proud of their new outlet on the sea. It had a new rail link with the coal and heavy industry of Polish Silesia, and it relieved Poland of her uneasy dependence on Danzig with its hostile German population. Gdynia was also a bolt-hole for the emigration of poor Jews. In new suits, black hats and side curls they queued up on the quayside with their families to be ferried by the Batory and Sobieski liners (built in Italian shipyards) to America, thus escaping, as it turned out, the horrors of the gas chamber.

The editorial policy of our magazine was to assert Poland's vital interest in Baltic and Scandinavian affairs, and to confront growing Nazi demands for territorial revision by asserting her rights to Upper Silesia, the Polish Corridor and in the Free City of Danzig (Gdańsk). Our contributors were mostly academics from Poland, Sweden, Finland and the three Baltic States. Much of the material was erudite and fascinating, some of it recondite – bee-keeping among the ancient Mordvinians, for instance, the function of chain-letters in Estonia, Lithuanian folklore. I polished up articles on the river routes through Russia taken by the Norsemen in opening up trade with Byzantium; on the role of Hanseatic grain exports, amber collecting, and the Baltic herring; on the spread of prehistoric Polish settlements beyond the Elbe unearthed by archaeologists; on skull measurement of Polish army recruits by Professor Jan Czekanowski (he found a substantial proportion of 'Nordic' types); on the incursions of the Teutonic Knights into Borussia and their shattering defeat at the battle of Grunwald (1410). There was some controversy over the spelling of place names – Wilno or Vilnius (Lithuanian), Cieszyn or Tešin (Czech) – which affected national susceptibilities. Piłsudski's seizure of Wilno (1920) had embittered Lithuanian relations with Poland, while the existence of the Corridor which severed East Prussia from the Reich seemed to the Germans an unbearable injustice.

One of our contributors was the Canadian Professor

William Rose of the London School of Slavonic and East European Studies, who had witnessed and written a study of the Upper Silesian plebiscite (1921). Two translators were kept busy with our Polish manuscripts: Bernard Massie, honorary consul in Poznań and a wounded war veteran, and Adam Truszkowski, who laboured for a pittance in a small Warsaw flat. Perhaps one of the criticisms of our magazine was that it lacked literary flair. Our academic contributors seemed to me to be rather a dull lot. I don't remember a single trace of humour in the volumes that I helped to edit. The magazine was set in old-fashioned linotype by a small Polish printer in Gdańsk, an hour or more's journey by train and tram from Gdynia. With the increase of political tension, Nazi louts began to molest our small Polish staff and we had to transfer printing to Bydgoszcz. Here I stayed at the Hotel Gastronomia, which served heavy meals of duck, dumplings and red cabbage. Even in Bydgoszcz, among a predominantly Polish population, Nazi propaganda was stirring up local Germans to intimidate Poles and provoke violence.

Café Mokka on the sea front in Gdynia subscribed to *The Daily Express*, and Beaverbrook's slogan on the front page 'There will be no more war' made the waiter laugh. The slogan implied that 'there will be no war as long as we look the other way and appease Hitler', which was a callous deception and encouraged the Nazis. By the end of 1938 my Polish friends advised me to see Warsaw before it was too late. Pat Howarth, who had been at Rugby and Oxford, and was later to continue working for the Poles as an army officer (SOE[1]) in Cairo, arrived to take my place. I had enjoyed my work, barking back at the Nazi propaganda machine (the Germans had opened their own rival institute in Königsberg) and I had by now strongly identified myself with Polish aspirations.

In Warsaw I took a job as English teacher at the Anglo-Polish School in Mokotowska. I had left behind the cold blustering winds that blew in from the Baltic for the monotony of snow-bound winter. Living in Gdynia, within a few miles of Nazi-held territory, in an enclave surrounded by Teutonic tribes, one had felt politically exposed. The fugitive Jews lining up on the Gdynia quayside to embark for New York must have had an instinctive feeling that they were getting away from their enemies just in time. In Warsaw, in the interior of Poland, one felt farther away from the threat of German panzers. Yet there was not much comfort in this, for Warsaw was nearer to the Russians and Russia too had its claims on Polish territory. No Pole would consider the notion of allowing a Russian army, even if it came as an ally, to set foot in Poland herself. For the Poles, Russia meant Bolshevism and Siberia.

The Anglo-Polish School was run by a Scotsman, Mackenzie. My pupils were mostly elegant housewives for whom the English classes were a novel social occasion. In Warsaw, as elsewhere in Poland, educated Poles had for generations preferred the politics and culture of the French, their intellectualism and revolutionary spirit. England, on the other hand, was thought of as a trading nation with colonies and a great navy but without the saving grace of Catholic faith. My pupils wanted to hear English spoken by a 'real' (prawdziwy) Englishman and asked me to read with them *Lady Windermere's Fan* and Dickens's *A Christmas Carol*. I had no literary qualifications and was probably a bad teacher. Private tuition brought in a little extra money. It meant tram journeys and hunting out middle-aged ladies who lived in old-fashioned flats along ill-lit corridors. My own digs were a bed-sitter on the corner of ul. Hoża and Marszałkowska. My landlady had been brought up in St Petersburg and spoke Russian. Her other lodger was a young man who was always behind with his rent. Every week-end she banged on his door. 'Łajdak!', she shouted. 'Bandyta! Cham! Open up. Pay me or leave my house.' I never met the young man, because he left one day without warning, taking with him the key.

My room had a great tiled stove, a brass bed and a dramatic painting of the Tsar's mounted Cossacks charging a crowd of Polish citizens in Warsaw during the rising of 1836. An iron balcony let in the morning sun. From it I looked down on rattling cabs – the hooves rang sharply on the cobble stones – and a throng of hawkers, drunks, army officers in capes, Jews – some in long gabardine coats and high boots wearing fur-lined hats – peasant women selling apples and flowers, and graceful girls with shapely legs. Despite the distractions of life in the capital, the films, theatre, concerts and cafés, the Paris fashions and opulent furs, there was underneath it a sense of tension. At night black-out exercises with Polish bombers circling overhead were a constant reminder of the threat of war. The Poles had little doubt by now that the Germans intended to attack their frontiers. The prospect of war seemed to stimulate rather than alarm them. Then on 31 March 1939, soon after the Germans marched into Prague, the situation was dramatically changed with the announcement by Chamberlain of Britain's unilateral guarantee of Poland's frontiers. The Poles, no longer on their own in a precarious no-man's land, now felt assured of the support of a great power, and my own status changed too from a humble teacher of English to an honoured ally. Waiters, cab drivers and shop assistants began to show me unusual politeness. Mr Mackenzie's school also benefited from a new influx of pupils, many of them enterprising young people who wanted to learn English to improve their pay and chances of promotion. Meanwhile in the spring and early summer sunshine Warsaw cast off its wintry look and rejuvenated itself. The bare trees which had stood like witches' brooms put on leaves, children came out to play in the parks and the benches in Łazienki Gardens were filled with people turning their pale, winter faces to the sun. I often sat at the foot of Chopin's monument with a book and a bag of cherries. English books were scarce: the most popular English author seemed to be Jack London – a Californian!

A much loved Englishman in Warsaw was Egerton Sykes. A non-stop talker, he spoke fluent Polish and acted as a sort of honorary cultural attaché. He organised Anglo-Polish social events and ran a newspaper, the *Warsaw Weekly*, which carried a bizarre advertisement for a special brand of bicycle saddle. Sykes was also a world expert on the mysteries of Atlantis. At one of his parties Noel Coward, who was a guest, asked me where I came from. 'Birmingham', I said. He looked disappointed and turned away. When summer came I joined two lodgers in a flat near Płac Trzech Krzyzy (Three Crosses). Franek was an overweight idler, Gandhi a toothless painter. Our landlady Pani Drabikowa was the widow of a well-known theatre artist. The flat was hung with his pictures, one of which showed Falstaff looking like a Polish nobleman of the 18th century with a wide sash and eagle nose. About this time I met Wanda (Dunia) Leśmianówka, daughter of the poet Bolesław Leśmian who had recently died. Wanda had been very fond of him. 'My father used words like a magician', she told me. 'But he was entirely unpractical and never learned to handle money – he kept his earnings in a cupboard among jars of honey and stuffed into a pillow case.' His sudden death left his wife and two daughters very poor. 'He came home one evening looking tiny and grey,' said Wanda. 'We could see he was mortally ill. He died the same evening.'

Wanda was a regular member of the National Theatre cast in which she played minor parts. I began to escort her home from the theatre. Walking back at night through the dark streets to my digs among the stray cats and staggering drunks, I got to know the watchmen. To economise on tobacco they would – like most poor Poles – break a cigarette in two and smoke each half separately in a wooden holder. Some of them told me how they had fought in the great battle of the Vistula (1920) when Piłsudski had routed the Red Army from the gates of Warsaw. They still thought of the Russian Bolsheviks as Poland's real enemy. The stroż (night watchman) with his stave, the cab driver cracking his long whip and the dozorca (concierge) with his keys and red-rimmed eyes were among my favourite characters. It was as well to be on good terms with the concierge. From his stuffy little lodge at the entrance to each apartment block – the gate was closed at 10 p.m. – he checked visitors, turned away prostitutes, mediated in the quarrels of tenants, and spied for the police. Conspicuous among the throng promenading past the smart shops on Aleje Jerozolimskie and Nowy Świat were Polish army officers, especially those from the best Lancer regiments and with landed connections; they enjoyed an enviable prestige. In the night clubs and bars they sat with the prettiest girls. I used to go to the Pod Bukietem bar, which had discreet cubicles. Café Krysztal had a string orchestra and was a place where business men went to pick up shop girls.

A notable feature of Warsaw was the high proportion of Jews. Their success as lawyers, doctors, academics, artists and as prominent members of the intelligentsia caused some envy and resentment among non-Jews. The great mass of Warsaw Jews, however, lived in poverty in crowded ghetto-like slums. They spoke Yiddish – an old and mixed German dialect characterised by its black humour – and retained their old customs, dress, trades and rituals. Like their compatriots in the neighbouring Russian Pale, they stubbornly resisted, under their rabbis, any attempt at assimilation. In a sense they were the poor relations left behind by those who had been enterprising or lucky enough to migrate to the West – to the Rhineland, London's East End, South Africa and America.

July 1939 was a month of glorious summer weather, and a sort of lull came over Warsaw. The last of the reserve officers, including Franek, had been called up, emptying the cafés. Jan Kipura, the singer, gave open-air performances to raise money for the air force; his appearance in the Rynek (Old Market) drew great crowds. Everyone sensed that war was coming, ('The Germans will attack once the harvest is in,' Gandhi warned me). Nevertheless the Poles kept their nerve. They had great faith in their own martial spirit, in their cavalry, and in the Allies' promises to come to their aid when the attack was launched. Poles had not grasped the new concept of *Blitzkrieg* in which fast-moving German Panzer columns with close air support were to thrust rapidly across frontiers. Stalin, it was thought, would stay out of a conflict and would certainly not cooperate with the 'Nazi Fascists'. No one, it seemed, had realised how difficult it would be, if not impossible, to get the French army to stir out of the Maginot Line or for the British Air Force and Navy to give direct support to its faraway ally on the Vistula.

However, the uncertainties of the situation did not worry me. My plan was to spend my August vacation on a walking tour in the Galician Ukraine. The idea horrified Wanda and her mother and sister. 'A mad-cap scheme,' they said. 'Once among those Russians, we'll never see you again.' So Wanda and I decided to get married, and we moved for a few days to a farm at Piekiełko not far from Warsaw on the local Samowarek (Puffing Billy) line. The farmer was a German 'colonist' from Swabia, with a Polish wife. He had been a soldier in Turkey under General Liman von Sanders, and showed me a photograph of himself in the Kaiser's uniform and a fez sitting on an Ottoman divan. Hired Ukrainian labourers, brown as gypsies, were bringing in the harvest. They slept in a barn with ikons, and sang endlessly to an accordion. It should have been a summer idyll. But people remarked that the planet Mars was glowing ominously red. After dark, searchlight beams flickered across the sky, and above the clamour of crickets we could hear soldiers' songs from a nearby camp, and the rattle of Polish army Fiat lorries.

In mid-August I took Wanda to the Carpathian Mountains where I intended to do some hill-walking. We awoke from an all-night train journey to find ourselves in a colourful and romantic world of golden maize and sun flowers, of garishly painted cottages and small wooden churches with a double-barred Orthodox cross on top of a cupola. Then on 23 August, while we were drinking wine with the landlord of an inn a few miles within the Roumanian[2] border, there came a shattering blow. A voice on the radio announced that Hitler and Stalin had signed a non-aggression pact. My first thought was that Poland was doomed. This was an act of direct treachery. It exposed Poland's eastern flank, gripping her in giant pincers. We hurried over the border back to Poland and in Kuty I was just in time to hear the town crier thump his drum outside the town hall and announce that German aircraft were attacking Poland's frontiers, and that Poland was at war. Huculi highlanders in smocks and thonged moccasins began to crowd the village squares, waiting for call-up instructions. I went to Kołomyja to find out the news, and was passing a Jewish shop when the owner called me over to join some men bending over a radio. Faraway I heard the voice of Chamberlain announce that Britain was now at war. A crowd had gathered round the British Embassy in Nowy Świat. After a few words from the British Ambassador, and Colonel Beck's reply, there were cries of 'Kochana Anglia!' and the strains of 'God Save the King'. One by one the people in the shop came up and shook my hand. I was no longer a voyeur. With this gesture I had become committed to being a participant in Poland's national drama.

Soon after this the first car-loads of refugees with baggage began to arrive from Cracow[3], Łódź and Warsaw on their way to Roumania. These were mostly professional people and intellectuals who possessed the means and initiative to escape. They had smeared their cars with mud as camouflage against German bombing. A woman who had been in charge of a Girl Guides camp on the Slovakian border told me that German tanks had raided the villages without warning and opened fire on people who were unaware that war had been declared. Trains were being bombed and passengers who fled into the fields were machine-gunned. As there were no communications or public transport, Wanda was unable to get in touch with her mother and sister in Warsaw[4]. Meanwhile the villages were filled with rumours. People looked up at the cloudless sky hoping to see the vapour trails of the RAF. But there was no news from the Allies. Shortly before the Russians marched in on 17 September 1939, we learned from an official at the voivodstvo (town hall) that Red Army troops were massing near the border and it would be unsafe for Wanda and me to stay. So we packed our fibre suitcase and walked over the Dniestr footbridge at Zaleszczyki into Bukovina (Roumania). It was a moment of humiliation. I was in flight. But the middle-aged Polish frontier policeman who stamped our passports gave me a challenging look, and said, 'Panie profesorze, niech pan wróci bombowcem' – 'When you return to Poland come back in a bomber.' Two days later we travelled from Czernowic to Bucharest in a train packed with Polish refugees.

During the war years I managed to retain my Polish ties. In Bucharest the British Council gave me a teaching post at the Commercial Academy, and I was in touch with many Polish refugees who were using Roumania as a staging-post before travelling to the West. Much of this exodus consisted of soldiers and airmen en route to join General Sikorski's Polish forces in France. Bucharest at this time, with its rumours, tension and frivolity was the setting for Olivia Manning's *The Balkan Trilogy*; Olivia and her husband Reggie Smith (the exasperating 'Guy Pringle' of her novels) were among my British Council colleagues. When France collapsed, the British military attaché (I was in the officers' emergency reserve) instructed me to join a party of British engineers whose mission, to sabotage the Roumanian oil fields in the event of German invasion, had been called off, and we left Constanza, watched by the local German consul, who waved goodbye, in an old Jewish cargo boat bound for Istanbul and Egypt. Soon I was back again with Polish friends. After a short infantry training course at Moascar bar-

Denis Hills

racks I was issued with a topee and bed-roll and sent off on attachment as liaison officer to Kopański's Carpathian Brigade, which was manning a sector of pill-boxes at Dikheila as part of the defences of Alexandria. This was a unit of adventurous spirits with a strong cavalry tradition. Some had escaped on skis from Poland over the Tatra mountains, others had broken out of internment camps in Slovakia and Hungary. They had regrouped in Syria. But when France fell they had defied the Vichy authorities' orders to surrender their weapons and accept internment and had made off with their equipment to Palestine, thence to Egypt. They had brought horses with them and galloped over the sand dunes in riding boots and breeches.

My next post with the Poles was as liaison officer to the Polish Officers' Legion which was camping west of Alexandria. The Legion was composed of some 200 spare reservists whom the Carpathian Brigade, now in Tobruk, was unable to absorb. Many of them were later usefully employed as administrative officers in occupied territories such as Ethiopia. Then in February 1942 we had sensational news. Stalin, in consequence of the German army's penetration into the Caucasus and a critical shortage of food supplies, had agreed to release thousands of Poles from internment camps in the USSR and to transfer them to British command. Within a few months 120,000 Polish soldiers and dependents were shipped across the Caspian and transferred to camps in Iraq and Palestine. Many were suffering from the after effects of malaria, typhus and malnutrition. A large number were camp followers: women and children, cabaret artists, ballet dancers, actors and musicians, ageing intellectuals and Jews (two of whom – Menachem Begin and the London rent racketeer Rachmann – were to become notorious). The first task was to weed out the dependents and unfit. The remainder were organised, at first in Iraq, into a corps of two infantry divisions and an armoured brigade with supporting arms and services under General Anders. I was attached to 5th Kresowa Infantry Division and was happy to sew the divisional sign, a brown bison, on my battle-dress sleeve. My Polish batman, a peasant from Białystok, promised to give me a plot of land when we marched back to Poland as victors. One day, pointing to some starlings which had appeared in our camp at Khanaqin, he said, 'They are Polish birds and have followed us all the way from Poland.'

It took a year to equip and train Anders's corps. By the time they embarked for Italy, the coastal strip from Gaza to Tel Aviv had been turned into a Polish enclave, with a high level of cultural and educational activities. Soon after they had arrived in Italy, the Poles were asked to play a key part in the final Allied offensive in May to capture Cassino and thus open the road to Rome. I remember well the night when I accompanied the first Polish troops of the 6th Lwowska Brigade to take over forward positions from Inniskillings of the 78th (Battleaxe) Division. Under heavy shelling and mortar fire the men (all freshly shaved) crept silently into caves and dug-outs, some of which were only a few yards from the enemy. From the burned, stony slopes of Cassino, littered with old corpses, the Poles went on to capture Ancona and Bologna. But they had, alas, to swallow two bitter pills. First, the news that the Warsaw rising of August-October 1944 had failed, with terrible destruction of life and buildings; second, the Yalta conference of February 1945, which agreed to the loss of Poland's eastern territories to the Russians. Many of Anders's soldiers came from east Poland. If they returned home they would lose their Polish identity and become Soviet citizens under Communist dictatorship. Faced with a choice of going back to face trouble as 'renegade Fascists' or building a new life in Britain or the Commonwealth, the overwhelming majority opted for the latter course. Out of a total strength of 112,000, only a few officers and just over 14,000 men chose to be repatriated to Poland. In May 1946 I stood on the quayside in Naples watching the last of them mount the gangway of a Liberty ship that was to take them back to Gdynia. They had stuffed their kit with spare socks, blankets and boots. No one cheered. They knew that a precarious future was waiting for them.

---

1   Special Operations Executive. (ed.)
2   'Roumania' (and 'Rumania') were spellings used before the War. Elsewhere in this text the name will be spelled Romania, as current now. (ed.)
3   The spelling often used before the War. Elsewhere in this text the name will appear as it written now, 'Kraków'. (ed.)
4   We were not to meet again until 1946, when they were traced to a Polish Red Cross camp in Porto San Giorgio. During the War they had worked in a Nazi forced labour factory in Austria.

Witold Ostrowski

Stalinism and After

Contacts between the British Council and the newly-founded Department of English at the University of Łódź began about 1947 when I was working with Professor Tadeusz Grzebieniowski as a senior assistant there. English studies had started in Łódź in 1946 from practically nothing, and we badly needed books and people to help us set up our programme. I remember some British Council people coming every fortnight or so from Warsaw to assist in training the students.

There was a tall middle-aged lady, slightly awe-inspiring, whose name, unfortunately, escapes me. (I am eight-four now and have a fairly good memory but only a few written records to aid these reminiscences). There was Mr C. McGahan, who later became a permanent member of staff and professor in Cracow[1]. There was the quiet Mr Innes, whose first name I forget, and the jovial Mr Jack Paul, a representative in Warsaw, whom we treated as a personal friend and whom I corresponded with privately after his retirement until his death.

The post-War years were a time of restoration and rehabilitation, but the Stalinist period was close at hand. The shock came in 1949 when Mr George C. Bidwell, another BC representative in Warsaw, denounced the Council as an instrument of espionage and asked for political asylum and Polish citizenship. The Council was silent about the *affaire*[2]; so were we Polish Anglicists, for no one really knew what reasons or aims might be concealed behind that spectacular act. It coincided with a thwarting of English studies.

A period of lull and hibernation set in for departments of Modern Languages and Literature throughout Poland. Exceptions were the departments at Warsaw and Cracow where studies had already been suspended officially – for want of qualified staff, it was said, though many people saw political motivation in this decision of the Ministry for Higher Education. It was not until the political thaw came in 1956 that the Ministry allowed the Department at Łódź to reopen. A few years after that we got our first permanent British Council lecturer in the person of Derwent May, a lean, sensitive, quick-witted scholar and author who taught with us for four years, married our best student and later, after setting up a happy family in Albany Street, London, continued to maintain friendly contacts with us.

Derwent May's engagement at Łódź coincided with a parallel engagement of an American visiting professor, sought out for our department by the cultural attaché of the US Embassy. The Americans were usually linguists, for in those times linguistics and applied linguistics had their period of violent growth in America. The British by contrast were generally content to stick with what they knew better, the literary tradition – which was to our satisfaction. Derwent May's stay of four years was exceptional. Normal contracts were for two years – in those times, the Council used to classify countries into categories of high and lesser risk and, after two years of hard life in a 'high risk' posting, more comfort and relief were generally offered. Our BC lecturers usually came to Poland after having served time somewhere in Libya or Indonesia; from Poland they were often promoted to a Western venue.

On our side a lot was done to attract these lecturers. They were contracted by both the Council and the University and were paid by both sides, so that about half of their salaries could be put aside in pounds sterling. They received one and a half times the salary of a Polish professor, plus a furnished flat. Though they were expected to pay the charges for telephone and organize their own board, their expenses were minimal and mostly taken care of. Warsaw as the capital city had its special attractions; Cracow with its medieval architecture presented other charms; but Łódź, a big drab city akin to Manchester or Leeds, was in those times especially unattractive. So when I succeeded my predecessor as Head of Department in 1964, I did my best to create a friendly atmosphere and good conditions for our foreign colleagues.

The flats they were given had much more room than we Poles could ever dream of. Polish colleagues undertook to treat them as friends and invite them to informal visits in their homes. My wife and I used to take special interest in how they were faring during our short Christmas and Easter vacations and would ask them to meals to celebrate those occasions. As my wife is an excellent housewife and cook and our hospitality was extended also to American visiting lecturers and British Council Directors and American cultural attachés, our home became known for its good food and friendly atmosphere.

Some foreign colleagues liked to spend their vacations in Warsaw or to go back to Britain. I managed to wheedle the passport authorities into granting them on arrival yearly triple-return visas so that they might come and go freely without having to repeat applications. I also encouraged lecturers to pursue their research, sometimes lightening their teaching burden so that they could do so; and I took care that they might publish their papers in our university journals.

From what I have said so far, it will be obvious that in those times of Communist rule the political aspect of teaching in Poland was highly important. British colleagues came usually indoctrinated by reading G. Orwell's *1984*; but after talks with their predecessors and the BC officers, their fears were generally tempered down. Probably they were instructed to be careful in what they said, and there was a tacit agreement between them and me to avoid discussing politics. My own position was of course difficult. It was assumed that people in superior positions in Communist countries were Party members; I was not. But being a public servant (for the University was a state university), I had to be loyal at least to the letter of the law, while at the same time trying to act for the real benefit of English studies and Polish humanities and culture.

To adapt oneself to these conditions and to our organization of studies was not easy for all of those who came to us in those decades. Usually the first year would be a time of learning and only in the second year did one get to normal knowledgeable work. As there was little opportunity for lecturers to organize classes in their own way with first and second year students, foreign colleagues were generally assigned tasks to do with the fourth and fifth years. Student attendance was an absolute requirement even at these levels, and we had to instruct our foreign friends to check lists and maintain discipline. Some of them wished to treat the students as equals or would succumb to the normal tendency of young students to try to lure the 'freshman' professor into teaching Practical English in a café or a park, or going to the cinema to see a British film – practices which might have triggered disciplinary procedures.

The duties of our BC lecturers were manifold. They were expected to teach and train; to serve as living models of Standard English; to act as authorities and advisors for the staff in the niceties of English usage; to read our research papers in English and suggest corrections. They acted as real intermediaries between the Department and the Council in Warsaw, and they tried to look after the interests of both institutions. Usually they did it admirably well. In one case only did I have to remind one of them that he was not solely an employee of the Council.

Owing to the lecturers and to general care from the Council, our departmental library received gifts of books from Britain and from the US numbering about 10,000 by 1964. We would also get newspapers like *The Manchester Guardian Weekly* and *The Times Literary Supplement*. Such donations were subject to political censorship; but fortunately for us, the power of censuring books was delegated by the University to a departmental commission, of which only one was a Party member, and a rather tame one at that.

Another important activity of the Council lecturer was to help us obtain long- and short-term scholarships for members of staff to Britain. Staff had no future if they did not prepare their doctoral theses, and without going to London or Oxford they would have no real access to the texts they needed. No British or American books could be bought in bookshops in Poland or ordered from foreign publishers; even the University Library had difficulties in importing them. The official channels through which Heads of Department were allowed to approach the Council in Warsaw were through the University to the Department of Academic Studies of the Ministry for Higher Education and then through the Department of Foreign Relations of the same to the Council, a machinery which was heavy, rusty, slow and not interested in sending people abroad, except if it were the Ministry's own people. In addition, there was a Ministerial official of whom it was said that he would simply not act. In these circumstances only a private visit by me to the Council in Warsaw, followed by quick mediation of the BC lecturer to put a check on the Council's own bureaucratic inertia, could get the job done. – Things moved well only when we acted together behind the scenes.

I remember names of ten BC lecturers in Łódź, all of them quite different. I was lucky if I could choose one with the highest academic qualifications and experience, but often it was Hobson's choice, because the British imagined Poland to be Orwell's nightmare, whereas the country was not so bad after 1956, with Marxist orthodoxy gradually spending itself in opportunism and the country becoming (as the saying went) like a radish – red on the outside, but white in. Only two of our lecturers, a man and a woman, were real and dangerous nuisances. Each of them was a kind of aggressive pioneer of the sexual revolution of the 1960s, possibly acting under the delusion that Communist rule was incomplete without change in morals and manners. They shocked some of our girls, demanding from them description of some masterpieces of European painting presenting nudes; and that was their least sin. I had to explain to them that if *Lady Chatterley's Lover* were to be read in class, the lot of English Studies in Łódź would probably be doomed. After an initial year, I told the Director of the Council in Warsaw why I did not want to see them again; he agreed with me, and we did not prolong their contracts.

The majority of the lecturers, however, were understanding, broad-minded people who strengthened our staff with their knowledge, ability and application. I especially treasure in memory James Clark, who unfortunately worked with us only one year (1968-9). He was a lively scholar, loved for his energy and sense of humour by both staff and students. With a team of the latter, he wrote and staged a Christmas pantomime about Robin Hood, which included a number of topical allusions and was a tremendous success. Another good friend of the Department was John Atkins who, like Derwent May and by the permission of the

Council, was allowed to prolong his and his wife's stay in Łódź to four years (1969-74). He is author of several books on modern British writers and his wife an artist-painter. He also produced a play in English, which was one of the practices of our Department in those days. I corresponded with him for some years after he retired.

In 1997, I received a large coloured photograph presenting the happy moment of congratulations offered by a dignitary of the University of Liverpool to our former Council lecturer Michael Parker. This was on the occasion of his being awarded a doctor's degree. In ceremonial togs and radiant, happy smile, he looked like what he is: the head of a department of English in a big comprehensive school, the author of a book on Seamus Heaney, the editor of an anthology of short stories on the Irish troubles and a poet. Following his time in Łódź, Michael married a Polish graduate student in English from the University of Warsaw and founded a happy family with three daughters in Cheshire. He learned enough Polish to be able to translate Polish poetry into English and from time to time, with his family, pays visits here.

At present writing (September, 1998), several British teachers are engaged in the Institute of English Studies at the University of Łódź. By the joint efforts of the British Council and the University, a British Reading Room and Lending Library has been open to the public for a number of years. These things demonstrate, I think, how our common enterprise in promoting English in Poland has not been in vain.

---

1   See Denis Hills's essay, note 3. (ed.)
2   See Derwent May's and Michael Irwin's essays for further reference to this event. (ed.)

Frank Tuohy

Setting up in Kraków

Iarrived in Poland in 1958 and spent two academic years as a
visiting professor at the Jagiellonian University in Kraków. I
returned in 1961 for a summer school and to do a bit of research
for the novel I was by then writing. My motives for going to
Poland were entirely based on curiosity and the desire to find a
subject to write about. This last I found and will always be grateful for this reason.

It is rather difficult to remember now how much people
gave the Communist régimes of East Europe the benefit of a considerable number of doubts. In England, if you supported the
Labour Party, you still tended to believe that there could be no
enemies on the left. Orwell and Koestler had both been acclaimed but had produced no great diminution in the number of fellow
travellers. As a writer of fiction, I was patronized at the time by
C. P. Snow and his wife Pamela Hansford-Johnson, who made
frequent visits to Moscow to be acclaimed and to pick up their
royalties. They informed one that in twenty years' time the two
great powers would come to resemble one another in wealth and
amenity so that there would be no choosing between them. I had
been living in South America where the rich intellectuals, known
as the 'festive left', frequently visited Communist countries and
came back with glowing reports. The same situation obtained in
Paris, where I had recently spent most of a year.

All this provided a motive for taking a look for oneself. In
Brazil there had been a large Polish colony: I had had several
students of Polish origin, and a Polish cook. I wrote in one short
story about an English girl married to a Pole that 'in those days
going to Poland seemed like walking off the edge of the world'.

Nevertheless, Polish acquaintances were always considering the idea of revisiting the homeland, though preferably when shielded by foreign passports. One friend, a barrister, kept receiving seductive nude photographs of his wife, not seen since 1939, with which she hoped to lure him back to Warsaw. He did not go. Later, in London, a publisher tried to put me off by referring to a successful novel called *The Visitors* (later a TV serial). It had all been done before, he said.

Before the days of the Wall you went by train through Berlin and after an interminable journey reached Kraków. (These train journeys came to be a part of one's life: the natives got through them by patrolling the corridors on the look out for a game of bridge or chess).

On arrival, the culture shock was pretty violent. I was met by one of my future colleagues, an English lady of academic bent and spartan disposition, later a valued friend, who had met her Polish husband in 1938 and survived it all since then. She took me to the Francuski Hotel, just inside the walls of the old City, where I was to live for about six months.

The Francuski was luxury by contemporary standards, but it was a gloomy place which ordinary Poles did not care to enter. Deputations of the Party faithful from neighbouring countries ate in the restaurant, their tables decorated with their countries' flags. A piano trio played extremely badly – they were rumoured to be retired members of the UB, the secret police. On every floor, Westerners were installed in bedrooms ending with the number 2, indicating that they were wired up. When I later met the lady who had taught English to the secret police, I was not convinced that their knowledge would be adequate to follow a conversation. My room was searched fairly frequently; I don't smoke, and fag ends would be left in the ashtrays. When I found the searchers *in flagrante*, I complained but I can't say I seriously minded. After six months I moved to a new apartment in the suburb of Bronowice, at the end of the tramline. The walls were thin, and one heard quarrels and children screaming a lot of the time: I was alone in a flat which otherwise would have held five or six people. A woman who worked in the Orbis travel agency had a flat on the ground floor of the building opposite. She was well-placed to see the coming and going of any visitors I might have.

The English department at the University was opened in 1958 with fifteen students in the first year. Another fifteen were added the following year, so that they numbered thirty by the time I left. Besides the Englishwoman already mentioned, two young Poles, a man and a woman, and myself made up the teaching staff. Later, another young woman joined us. I liked them all, but I am afraid our approach to the job in hand was somewhat amateurish. We were finding our way. The only problem we did not have was that of enormous numbers.

Poland adhered to the continental European tradition, also to be found in the United States, in which the professor sweeps in, delivers his lecture to a packed audience and sweeps out again. Communication with students, if it takes place at all, is made through assistants and graduate students. We had the opportunity for personal contact with our students and I took to giving supervisions or tutorials to fill up the afternoons when time was heavy on one's hands. Partly this was due to fond memories of Cambridge where such contacts were more important than lectures, which I had very rarely attended. Partly it was because I put the ability to write and understand English before the communication of over-simplified half-truths about writers whom none would get around to reading. Thus I made no collections of howlers about *King Lear* or *Tess of the D'Urbervilles*, but tried to make students write English reasonably clearly. In those first two years there was not very much further one could go.

The tradition in Kraków was Germanic, philological, linguistic. Opposition to opening up the Department had not only come from those who feared a threat to compulsory Russian and the political implications thus involved. There was also hostility from a scholar who believed no one should learn English without first having mastered Anglo-Saxon. Among the professors we had a 'godfather' to look after us with an alert and benevolent eye: he was an internationally renowned linguistician, whose distinction and detachment had given him the freedom to travel overseas. (When I told him about my room at the Francuski being searched, he said: 'Of course, the same thing happened to me in

London, but it is the wrong thing to do.') On one occasion he nearly missed a conference in Dublin, the Republic of Ireland then only recognizing the exiled Polish government in Kensington. The British Embassy came to the rescue; something was cooked up and our friend was able to give a much acclaimed speech – in Irish, of course. He was believed to speak seventy-two languages. Another professor of philological bent was an expert on Bushman Clicks, which he imitated on a violin. Examples like these gave one a feeling of the atmosphere of the University. In spite of atrocities such as the shooting of half the professors by the Germans in 1939 and the later imposition of Communist control, a reasonably independent traditional existence seemed to have survived behind the scenes. Few of the professorate were Party members: at a guess, there were probably more of those at Oxford or Cambridge in those days.

Until the opening of the English department the teaching of English, as a third language after Russian, had been in an organisation called, I think, the Studium, which provided English teachers for the other departments in the University. This was run by a lady very much a Party member of the New Class, though rumour had it that she had been seen at prayer in one of Kraków's many churches. The teachers under her were a picturesque group. I got to know them by being asked to address them once a week on points of language they brought up. Some were Americanized returned émigrés, but those most vivid in memory belonged to the former upper class. These ladies had been educated abroad between the wars or earlier, some of them alumnae of organizations like the Order of the Sacred Heart, a worldwide mafia which includes ex-President Cory Aquino of the Philippines and the Empress of Japan. They spoke English and French, and probably German, with confidence and without bother, effectively making one's own insistence on grammatical niceties seem irrelevant. They were great party throwers and party goers and offered a social life which it was difficult, in the circumstances, to refuse.

Such survivors, I believe, were obliged to live in Kraków rather than Warsaw. In any case this was a city of art, of art historians, and with jobs in museums and libraries. It was a centre for the Catholic intelligentsia, who supported a much

Frank Tuohy

censored magazine which survived through the most difficult years. Often I was ill at ease in the *bien pensant* atmosphere, having Catholics on one side of my family and having observed the faith in action, or rather in inaction, in South America before the days of Liberation Theology. I felt the Kraków intellectuals were not looking for intellectual freedom. Poland had a conflict between two ideologies and theirs was the clear winner, even then. The churches were crowded each Sunday. Oppression had given a cutting edge to faith (Kraków produced a Pope not long afterwards). I remember one of these devout ladies wailing to the American cultural attaché: 'They must give us back religious education in schools, like in America!' 'But we don't have that in America', he replied. She did not believe him.

A friend brought up as a Protestant told me how much she had suffered prejudice from not belonging to the majority. But another minority had suffered far worse. When you were talking to somebody and you mentioned a third person, your interlocutor immediately informed you if that person was Jewish. Is this anti-Semitism? It happened all the time. In the English Department I put up a notice: 'There's one subject we don't discuss here'. But we did: we couldn't avoid it and if the devout lady disbelieved the cultural attaché, for her his race would have been sufficient reason.

The first students in the English Department had already been selected by my English colleague. I realised later that it was a difficult task, well done: there were few duds in that inaugural year. As usually happens in university courses, however, there was a wide spectrum of knowledge. Four or five could speak pretty fluently and wore the typical ironic know-all student expression as one laboured to explain something to the less proficient of their classmates. One girl was quite exceptional. I had smuggled in a copy of *Dr Zhivago*, at that time a hot property, banned in Poland. She read it over a weekend and delivered a ten page essay by Tuesday.

A young man of supreme self-confidence made himself quickly unpopular with the others: he was the type that sits in the middle of the front row and sticks up his hand when you ask someone else a question. Without definite proof, we suspected that he was our link with Authority. He was quick to latch on to foreign visitors, to help them buying black market Russian cameras and in other slightly shady activities, which tended to be part of the normal transactions of Polish life, but were perhaps unwise for British Council visitors. When I warned some Americans against him at a summer school, I was snubbed. The trouble was that visitors to Communist countries got a bit exalted, deriving some sort of 'high' on conspiracy theories, and this could be infectious.

The entrance examinations in the second year gave an insight into the unseen pressures and subterranean workings of this deeply contradictory society. For some time before, the Department received letters requesting 'protection' for various candidates who would be coming before us. Some of these came from the Party, others from relations or religious affiliations. I asked not to be shown any of them, or to be told about them. I was beginning to feel the undertow, the drift away from judicious detachment, which always accompanies personal involvement in an alien society. It was the first time I'd come across 'affirmative action', then a concept scarcely formulated in Western countries. Our academic standards had been formed by the students we already had in the first year. But accompanying each new candidate was a dossier often devastating in its implication: war orphans, children born in concentration camps or exiled from the areas of Polish expansion in Lithuania or the Ukraine. Sadly, one after another of these failed to come up to scratch; others considered socially advantaged were far better prepared (private lessons from the polyglot ladies of the 'Studium'). One threw up one's hands in despair or, in my case, got the worst migraine I had ever experienced. Here in affirmative action, one was at the centre of the whole socialist ideal, its blundering, passionate and genuine desire to help in this world rather than in the hereafter. At the same time, one remembered those requests for 'protection', which sabotaged the system.

It was hard to tell how much the students at the University went along with all this. For them applying for Party membership was just a career move. On Tuesdays the men were supposed to do military service. You were told the way to dodge this was to buy a tin of Nescafé on the black market and drink

Frank Tuohy

the lot. This created palpitations which led to medical rejection. I used to watch the survivors being drilled from my window in the English Department, a bedraggled troupe of jokers falling in, falling out and falling over. It was somehow encouraging.

One learned a good deal from the British students on Polish government scholarships. One, in particular, an architect from Glasgow, was at first enthusiastic. Later, he was 'approached' and this caused him to change his mind. The other student also was 'approached', the aim, presumably, being to get foreign students to report on each other's activities. Tactlessness and boasting could endanger one's friends, as with the case of the son of two distinguished American writers who was later studying at the University. That, to my knowledge, was the only time the Secret Police the UB, or its successor, visited the English Department. But my colleagues would have kept such occasions from me.

Once the Department was opened, various people started working for doctorates. The problem was to choose an English or American writer agreeable to the authorities. One friend had done a considerable amount of work on Howard Fast, a novelist well known at the time. She was saddened when I told her that Fast had been for long expelled from the Party and was very much *persona non grata*. Later she ventured on composing a reader for use in schools; the publishers rejected this because her typical American family had a bathroom in their home, something untypical in Poland.

The question of books for study and research was a difficult and problematic one. As far as I remember there was a small nucleus of a library remaining from before the War, when a popular and celebrated professor, who wrote books about writers like Priestley and Charles Morgan, had headed the Department. Apart from that, we inherited some packing cases of works in English of obscure origin.

The Fine Arts Department at the University was in the charge of a hospitable and energetic professor who had spent the War in Britain. He belonged to the distrusted minority, as did his forceful lady assistant, and, as I suggested previously, people always let you know it. This rather distinguished man had headed a commission to trace and bring back works of art and the treasures which had been looted by the Germans. He had performed this task with gusto, so much so, he told me, that there were extra treasures of obscure provenance which he had included in his haul.

The pile of books which appeared in the English Department could have been the result of one of these expeditions. A large area of Germany had fallen into Polish hands and there must have been some remarkable items turning up. The books I inspected would have been pretty dull, because I remember nothing about them, except that several bore the bookplates of August Von Schlegel, the German translator of Shakespeare. Rootling among these obscure works, I found a slim leather volume of two pamphlets bound together. One was *Remorse*, a tragedy performed at Drury Lane in 1813, and the other was 'Christobel' [sic]. The latter had extensive corrections in the author's hand, and both had rueful dedications to Schlegel in an entirely characteristic style, with the writer lamenting that his inspiration had fled. They were signed S.T.C. It was an exciting moment. S.T.C. must be something of a patron saint to anyone who has ever struggled to communicate in gaps between drudgery, sloth and inanition. Each marginal annotation in ink the colour of dried blood, looked personal and significant. The question was what to do with this discovery.

I discussed the find with my colleagues. We were all against delivering the volume to the University authorities, after which it would have ended up neglected in a glass case. The next decision was my own, to export it to England during the winter vacation. In London I ended up at an antiquarian bookseller, where I was viewed with some suspicion. I explained too much, forgetting that in those days it was hard to communicate the paranoid atmosphere of Communist Europe to anyone outside. They retreated into an alcove, then emerged, impressed, and offered £300. It was not enough, but it was sufficient to equip the Department with standard editions of British writers. Before selling the book, I copied out the dedications and recorded the variant readings in 'Christabel'. In the 1960s my cottage in England suffered an inundation like the one in *The Mill on the Floss*, and my papers were reduced to papier mâché, these notes included.

Frank Tuohy

There was a stripped-down aspect of life in Poland which was in its way appealing. Very few people had any money. In the street you recognised your friends by the clothes they wore – they mostly had only one lot. After a winter through which cabbage and potatoes had been the chief articles of diet, spring arrived. It was like spring in wartime – you had almost forgotten that it could happen. Ancient survivors basked in the sunshine in the Planty, the public garden that replaced the walls of the old city.

Expeditions to the country were a return to the 19th century, with dusty roads, cornflowers and cockle among the crops, the smell of earth closets and horse manure. This last was supposed to benefit the strawberries, which tasted better in Poland than anywhere else.

My second spring in Kraków brought the opening of a British reading room in a building owned by the University, with books provided by the British Council. The building itself was an 18th century palace on the Planty and had belonged to an aristocratic family, whose last survivor, aged 90, lived upstairs. He lay in bed wearing a green skull cap, under a huge portrait of his mother, and recited poems which he had written in English. I remember them as being rather good. He was looked after by his butler, whose children were by now doctors and lawyers.

The Reading Room when it opened was full of the type of books – Durrell, Greene, Murdoch, Waugh – which my friends longed to read. In the Kraków fashion, it was looked after by an austere lady, a former margravine. On the day after opening, a snag arose: all visitors had to sign their names in a book. There was a unanimous outcry against this, and the place was thenceforward deserted. I don't know what happened later, because I had left the country.

It is an aspect of student life to feel always in the presence of the great problems of society and the future. In a Communist country, devoid of the temptations induced by a market economy, this feeling seemed to persist into the ordinary adult world. The unending presence of choices and decisions gave an intensity to one's existence there, the sensation of being locked up in the later chapters of a Dostoyevsky novel. Life in those two winters was drab in the extreme but one's memory tends to blot out the times of boredom and frustration. One remembers discussions of significance and forcefulness which were hard to find in later life. The energy and the passion which had survived years of tragedy and despair, proved to be rare in the comfortable trivial world of Western Europe. I have never been back, but I think I foresaw that liberation would always bear the prospect of disillusion.

Recently, I visited St Petersburg and an Englishman working there told me: 'The surprising thing is, these people are immensely well-educated!' I think the same was true of socialist Poland, even in the fifties, and it was fascinating to have been a witness of those times.

Author's note: I have used no proper names because of misspelling as well as discretion. Since writing these pages I have revisited Poland, but have seen no reason to alter the impressions recorded here.

Derwent May

Early Years in Łódź

I went out to teach English literature at the University of Łódź in October 1959. One day, after I had been at work for several months, a student asked if he could have a word with me. He led me to a quiet corridor. 'Mr May,' he said, 'I want to tell you that I have to go each month and report on you to the UB – the secret police. But' – and here he beamed broadly at me – 'I always tell them something nice about you!'

It was a touching episode for me – but it was also a very expressive example of the atmosphere in Poland at this time. The yoke of Communist authority still lay on every shoulder. However, under President Gomułka, who had come dramatically to power in 1956, it lay there a little more lightly than it had in the immediate post-War, Stalinist days. People were not so frightened and were beginning to speak more freely both among themselves and to foreigners. The fact that I was there in Łódź was a sign of this.

Everywhere in Poland, in fact, the major institutions were still staffed largely by men and women who did not believe in Communism – often people who had started their careers there before the War. Indeed the régime could not have creaked on, even as incompetently as it did, without their support. They went on working conscientiously for the sake of Poland and its people, not for Communism, although they were often obliged to be members of the Party. Now, with a skilled combination of tact and daring, they had begun to speak out. There was a brilliant sociology professor at Łódź University, who every year addressed his new students. 'I am here to help you, and I must tell you straightaway that you have two choices here. You can either be a sociologist or you can be a success. Whichever you decide, you will have my support.'

'Success' in Communist Poland did not depend very much on being an honest scholar, especially in a field that was so close to politics as sociology. The Party liked to hear noises that pleased it and promoted those who made them. But scholarship struggled on – as did wit and humour. I once asked a Warsaw literary critic how the idea of socialist realism was applied to music. For example, who were the socialist realist composers? He thought for a moment, then said, 'Those who're dead, and those who say they are'. In every sphere, the Communist system was one of farcical compromise between theory and reality – and Poles had a well-developed eye for the farcical.

The English Department at Łódź University was only a few years old, and at the time I arrived had not yet produced its first graduates. I had some learned and delightful Polish colleagues, mostly pre-War graduates of Warsaw University, who had set it up. But the five-year degree course that the students had to take was another compromise, and one that gave them a hard time. They found themselves ground between the Party and the old German-style academic traditions of Central Europe. The Party insisted that all undergraduate courses should include an examination on Marxism. The Party also wanted university degrees to be of some distinct utility – in this case, to provide a sound practical grasp of the English language, as well as of another language, which was generally French.

But pre-War traditions died hard in the academic world. So, as main subjects, the students had to do English philology both historical and theoretical (plus some Latin) and had to cover the whole history of English literature from the Anglo-Saxons to modern times, including American literature. This enormous programme meant that almost everything was in danger of being done superficially and by rote. In particular, 'history of literature' meant far more reading about authors than actually reading them.

I decided that the best contribution I could make was to concentrate on close, appreciative reading of poems and plays and novels, to try to bring them really to life for the students. It was a style of teaching they were not used to. At school, literature lessons consisted more often than not of long lists of names and plot-summaries and dates. I was given a wholly free hand within the broad outlines of the syllabus, and after the first shock I think many students began to appreciate this approach.

They needed a good grasp of the language for this, but most of them arrived at the University quite well prepared. To learn English had become a passion in Poland since 1956, and Łódź was full of private teachers coaching schoolchildren who were hoping for a place in the English Department. I taught wholly in English, as did my Polish colleagues. There were inevitably comic moments. Once, in a first-year oral exam on some set books, I asked a student why the artist-hero of Somerset Maugham's *The Moon and Sixpence* goes to the South Seas. 'Oh, to relieve himself, sir,' she said.

At Warsaw University, where I went every week to give a course on modern poetry to the fifth year, I was able to spend two months going line by line through T. S. Eliot's *The Waste Land* without the numbers falling off – and also to try another experiment. In general, I spoke about Jane Austen and Dickens, or about Yeats and Eliot, in just the way I would have done in Britain. Insofar as my comments on literature implied any wider political or moral point of view, it was a broadly liberal one. As an employee of the British Council, accepted by the Polish authorities, I felt it both legitimate and proper to take that tone, which came naturally to me. I did not pointedly contrast this approach with the more political, Marxist interpretation of literature that most of my students would have been taught at school (in some cases with conviction, more often perfunctorily or insincerely). All the same, I wanted them to notice the contrast – and of course they did, without any effort on my part.

One Friday evening in Warsaw I decided to go through a poem by W. H. Auden, 'The Unknown Citizen'. I stressed before I began that this poem was a supposed epitaph for one of its employees – 'JS/07/M/378' – by a large American corporation. So we began. 'He was found by the Bureau of Statistics to be/One against whom there was no official complaint.' They were already recognising the language. 'Our researchers into Public Opinion are content/That he held the proper opinions for the time of year;/When there was peace, he was for peace; where there was war, he went.' The point needed no further nudging by me. And when we reached the last two lines, some of them, I felt, did not know whether to laugh or cry: 'Was he free? Was he happy? The question is absurd:/Had anything been wrong, we should certainly have heard.'

Teachers are inevitably inclined to dwell on what they could do for their protégés. But here in Poland no foreign teacher could, I think, go on thinking in that way for long. Poles, young and old, had lived through so much tragedy and deprivation that one soon became the learner in practically every sphere of life.

Literature was no exception. Under the Gomułka régime, Polish poets, novelists, playwrights and film-makers were being given a little more freedom from the censor. One of the most stunning of the comically subversive playwrights, Sławomir Mrożek, whom I later came to know, gave me an account of a discussion about one of his plays at the Party Central Committee. Could they allow twelve performances of a new play he had written? No – that would be far too likely to inflame dissident youths and cause public disturbances. What about eleven then? Er – no, no, still dangerous. Ten? Yes, ten, that would be safe enough. Give him ten.

Mrożek's plays and stories were themselves mainly ironical portraits of such situations. They slipped past the Party by shooting their irony in all directions, so that the censor did not know quite what to make of them – like his story 'The Last Hussar', the tale of Bunny, who scrawls anti-Communist slogans in public lavatories, and when he thinks he has been detected and that all the public lavatories are being closed because of him, goes into the countryside and writes them with a stick in the snow.

Other writers, by now being allowed to publish small editions of their work, went beyond comic irony and absurdism. The poet Zbigniew Herbert was finding a tone of tragic irony to say something about the almost inexpressible: the German occupation, which had left almost no family in Poland without a victim. He was writing poems like 'The Stone', which has subsequently become well-known in the West. 'The stone,' he says, 'is a perfect creation': it is so dignified, so self-contained, so impervious to feeling – what more could a human being wish to be?

Łódź itself was a grim town to live in, an old cotton town known as 'the Polish Manchester', whose factories were still practically Victorian, pouring out smoke and smells. The long high-street contained some magnificent turn-of-the-century baroque facades, with heaving or elegant caryatids holding up grandiose balconies, but was smothered by a century of industrial grime. The city authorities had, however, ingeniously managed to preserve its pre-War name 'Piotrkowska' at the time when every High Street (or 'Ulica Główna') had to be renamed after Stalin: there was a little Ulica Główna that went back to the days when Łódź was still a village, and they got away with renaming that.

In the worst days of winter a kind of black linoleum of thawed and refrozen snow covered the streets; it creaked as you walked along. Spring came quite suddenly in mid-April. Almost overnight, the horse-chestnut trees were bursting into leaf – traditionally the moment when students began work for their examinations in June. One of the best new buildings in the city was the University library, where as they worked in May they could hear a nightingale – or to be wholly accurate, a thrush-nightingale, the related East European species – singing in the park below.

Ugly city though it was, the countryside seemed quite close in Łódź. Peasant women came to the door with necklaces of dried mushrooms hanging on them, or with baskets of wild strawberries; those from the Lowicz district still wore long skirts decorated with purple and yellow stripes, a design used by the local archbishop for his servants 400 years ago and borrowed from Michelangelo's designs for the Papal Guard in Rome. When I went to Warsaw, I often used to catch a fast train at six in the morning, and the station was always crowded with peasant farmers drinking steaming glasses of hot beer to keep out the cold.

Trams ran into the countryside on either side of the city, and one soon found oneself among the rye fields. They too shot up once mid-April was past; by May the rye had a purple bloom on it, which explained the old English song, now anachronistic, which ends with the lines, 'And Susie says she'll marry me when bloom is on the rye – oh, how I wish the blooming bloom was on the blooming rye.' By June the fields were being harvested; by

July, all that was left in them was a little square of barley, out in the middle – it ripened later than the rye, and was grown for the farmer's own use.

There were plenty of jokes to be heard about the countryside and the stubborn Catholicism of the peasants – rather like that knot of barley at the heart of the ryefields, I thought. One very Polish story was about the peasant woman who lost her cow, and went to church to pray to God to send her a new one. As she came out, the local Party secretary accosted her. 'It's no use going there for another cow. But I'll tell you what – the Party will give you half the cost of a new one, just to show you who you can depend on.' The woman rushed back into church. 'Punish the Party secretary for his wickedness, dear God. He's kept half of the money you sent me!'

Going by train up to Warsaw I often saw those precious solitary cows, with a boy or an old woman in attendance, devoting their day to its welfare like a cow's gentleman.

I lectured in Warsaw on Friday evening and Saturday morning, and usually stayed at the Bristol Hotel, where the receptionist, translating the Polish greeting rather literally, always greeted me as 'Sir professor', knighting and chairing me in one breath.

The Bristol was full of revelations. It has recently been thoroughly modernised and rebuilt, but when I was in Poland it still had all its pre-War fittings, such as mermaid door-handles which obliged you to rest your thumb on a naked breast. In the morning you would see well-off Poles having a leisurely breakfast in the main dining-room, often with a glass or two of vodka, while 'delegations' of ill-dressed Russian workers were speedily bustled through by the management to an out-of-the-way room at the back. In the evening the rather louche 'back bar' was where journalists and film people gathered. Polish journalists came there as well as foreign correspondents – they were all suspected of being informers, but no one bothered about them any more than I did about my student informer.

Government control of the press was very tight, and all the newspapers were packed with relentlessly good economic news and statistics. Poles were also, of course, fed with Party views not just for their own benefit but also because the newspapers had to present official policy to the outside world. Occasionally there were political topics on which there was not a firm Party line. One major event in which this was the case when I was there was the Algerian war. The Communist parties naturally had to support a fight for national independence against a colonial power, yet at that time the Russians were assiduously cultivating friendship with France and did not want to offend her. So Polish reporters were left to report objectively on what was happening, and the best Warsaw paper, *Życie Warszawy*, carried excellent despatches from Algeria – better even than those in the Western press outside France, because Poles made the most of their unaccustomed freedom.

Polish films had gone through a spectacular phase in the heady days just after Gomułka's rise to power in 1956, with the Andrzej Wajda masterpieces like *Ashes and Diamonds* in the forefront. Film-makers, like writers, still had a degree of independence but nothing quite so distinguished was being made now. I was invited to work on the English subtitles of one or two films, in collaboration with the excellent translator of C. P. Snow's novels, Cecylia Wojewoda. The best one that I did was a moving and ironic story about a man hiding in a woman's flat during the German occupation, Wojciech Has's *Jak być kochana* (*How to be Loved*), with Wajda's favourite star, Zbigniew Cybulski, as the man. Cecylia and I spent many hours together in Warsaw over scripts and in front of screens, and at one point I had to explain why we could not call a letter in French a French letter, but we got the job done in the end.

The Warsaw skyline was dominated wherever you went by the enormous, banal tower of the Palace of Culture – Stalin's 'gift' to Poland, and a permanent reminder to Poles that Russian might was not far away even when invisible. Poles used to say of the Palace 'It's tiny, but in such good taste'.

I had one comic reminder of this nearness of the invisible Russians, or at least of their surrogates the UB, when I went one day to the cinema with a Polish friend in Łódź. This friend, called Wojtek Lipiński, was an elderly man who had been in prison in the Stalinist days, simply because before the War he had been a young officer on the general staff of the army. He had spent the War in Scotland, but unlike most of the Polish soldiers who came to the United Kingdom, he had opted to go back home after VE Day – only to find himself flung almost immediately into gaol.

While he was in Britain, he had learned to speak English extremely well. In fact, he was one of the few Poles I met who, when speaking English, dropped their voice at the end of a sentence in the normal English way. In Polish the voice rises at the end of a sentence, but if English is spoken in this way it leaves an English listener on tenterhooks, because he is waiting for the signal that an utterance is over, and it never comes. This made Wojtek a refreshingly relaxing person to talk to. He was also very witty and ironical. He had been released from prison when Gomułka came to power, but would never forgive the régime, and refused all the compensation he was offered. He eked out a living giving English lessons in the Medical Department of the University.

We often met for lunch, and the police must have known all about our meetings, since we were both in principle suspicious characters. On the afternoon when we went to the cinema, someone must have heard an Englishman and a Pole speaking together in the darkened auditorium and thought it his duty to inform the authorities. As we came out with everyone else at the end of the film, there was a tremendous blare of police sirens, and two police cars screeched to a halt by the cinema entrance. I saw eight faces peer out of the car windows at the crowd. They saw Wojtek and me – and I saw eight faces fall in disappointment. It was just that damned May and Lipiński again!

I have been back to Poland once since those days. It was not long after the overthrow of Communism, but there was already a towering American-style hotel in the middle of Warsaw, and I was staying there. I arrived after dark and went up in the lift to my room on the top floor. The first thing I wanted to do was to look out on the lights of Warsaw and orientate myself. I looked up into the sky for the Palace of Culture – the natural landmark to start with. I could not see it, and was quite baffled. I looked down and there it was, a shrunken little building far below me. There could not have been a better symbol of Poland's new era of hope.

Michael Irwin

Through the Two-Way
Looking-Glass

Iwanted to keep this reminiscence objective, but found that I couldn't. Memories of Poland are too intimate and highly flavoured – family matters. Eventually it seemed more candid to leave my past self plainly in the account, as representing the film on which the snapshots were printed. In the years since I moved from Britain to Poland both countries have changed so radically that recollection has been discoloured by ironies and contradictions. It's hard to remember straight. In any case my experiences were conditioned by my expectations of a kind now obsolete.

I went to Poland in 1958, direct from university. As a grammar-school boy from Camden Town, viscerally left of centre, I hadn't much relished Oxford. It offered social privileges which I disapproved of and luckily didn't happen to enjoy. Keen to get far away from high tables, gowns, scouts and sconcing, I'd planned, with a school friend, to work six months in a factory to accumulate some money and then move abroad. We had India in mind because it seemed distant and exotic. (During National Service I'd applied for the Far East, but been consigned to Hereford).

My tutor, Nevill Coghill, who had always been generous to me although (I inferred) right of centre, cut across this plan with an unexpected offer. A medievalist from Poland, Professor Przemysław Mroczkowski, who was somehow contriving to spend a year in Oxford, had been looking for a lecturer to teach for a year at KUL, the Catholic University of Lublin. Would I be interested? I was, immediately. Geographically speaking, Poland might be a lot closer than India, but in other ways it seemed much further off – a mental space with remote frontiers, political, historical and cultural. It was also a little frightening. In those days few people went behind the Iron Curtain, and some of those found difficulty in re-emerging. There would be a whiff of Graham Greenery about such a visit. I talked to Professor Mroczkowski in his Oxford lodgings, and heard about the precarious, beleaguered existence of KUL in its hostile political context. It emerged that Graham Greene had in fact paid a recent visit... If this garrison needed whatever help a visiting English lecturer could offer it would be gratifying to provide it, especially since, as a lapsed Catholic, I felt a posthumous twinge of family feeling. I accepted Mroczkowski's offer, and my friend later went to India alone.

My ignorance about Poland was lavish, the few general ideas I could muster being centred around snow and Chopin. But I was aware that the country had acquired an intriguing new political status following the events of October, 1956[1], and the reinstatement of Gomułka. If some of the early euphoria had evaporated, it still seemed, at least from Britain, that there might be promise in a Polish version of Communism. Given what had happened to Hungary, of course, due allowance would have to be made for the need to withstand pressure from the Soviet Union. Political and social developments would have to be viewed with a tolerant, interpretative eye. Here was a country that had been shattered in the War and was only now getting the chance to reshape its own destiny.

Tolerance was taxed immediately by the very process of trying to gain admission to Poland. It had transpired that Professor Mroczkowski had recruited not only me but two other new graduates, Anne Hargest from Cambridge and Anita Jones from Durham. We were due to start work in Lublin in September and applied for visas in good time. But September came and went. So did October. The weeks of unemployment crawled. In November the three of us conferred about the possibility of pulling out but agreed to hang on a little longer. The visas were eventually granted in December.

We travelled together by train and were met in Warsaw not

Michael Irwin

only by Irena Przemecka, from KUL, but by the British Council representative – a kind gesture since our appointments had nothing to do with the Council. I'd barely heard of the organisation before, beyond the occasional denunciation in *The Daily Express*, but the hospitable greeting was very welcome after the thirty-six hour journey. We were able to freshen up in the Grand Hotel, the first hotel in which I'd ever set foot: it seemed the right privilege in the right place. Afterwards we went to the British Council headquarters opposite the then new Palace of Culture, the hated imperialist skyscraper rearing over the war-flattened town. Somehow the Council's office and library had survived the grim Stalinist days, though we were told that when things were at their worst, only the old had dared to go on making use of them. Now there was life and movement again. This was the first of many demonstrations Poland was to offer that in a totalitarian environment doggedness was a major virtue. Doors, windows, even loopholes, should be kept open wherever possible; something might one day get through.

Lublin proved to be a subdued provincial town without specialities. As in Warsaw the most obvious visual features were the new apartment blocks of raw, unfaced brickwork, like buildings that had been crudely skinned. Protruding from each were the metal sockets designed to hold flags on days of national rejoicing. Traffic was scanty, the shops had little to sell and the street-lamps were dim. There was a general frugality and colourlessness that recalled wartime Britain. Anne, Anita and I were housed in Chopin Street, where we each had a single sizeable room in a shared flat – shared, in my own case, with two priests. Visits to local people were soon to make us realise how privileged we were in terms of space and privacy.

In Lublin, as elsewhere in Poland, people had already lost most of their faith in Gomułka. Even under the new political dispensation, KUL proved to be subject to considerable pressure from the state. It was never clear from year to year whether a given discipline would be allowed to admit a fresh contingent of students for the following autumn. Various departments had already been phased out by a refusal. The expectation was that this process would continue; while the institution would not be closed down completely, it might by degrees be cut back to a mere seminary. A state university recently opened in the town was dilating as KUL contracted. Since moves were being made to found an English school in this university, the omens for the KUL department weren't good. In any case material conditions within it were spartan. The five-year degree boldly spanned the whole history of English literature, yet accommodation was scanty, books were desperately few, and stationery was grey and furry. Teaching tended towards methodological extremes: on the one hand the survey lecture about great works the audience had never read, on the other detailed study of the single poem circulated in stencilled copies. The students tended to be pale and prone to illness, sufficiently fed but insufficiently nourished. I was far enough away from the dinners in hall that I'd skipped at Oxford.

But it was plain then, and is with hindsight still plainer, that for all the material limitations the true essentials of a university department were there. The staff, mostly recent graduates, trained from the start by Mroczkowski, had acquired their qualifications in difficult days against strong odds. The Catholicism of the Catholic University didn't loom large in any institutional sense, but there was an almost religious conviction about the teaching, which Mroczkowski, a devotee of Newman, did much to foster. The staff set themselves high academic standards, knew their students well and nurtured them. Though a lot of work was done, the atmosphere was friendly and familial: you knew everyone's name. There would be departmental picnics, dances, drama productions and parties – at which Mroczkowski, by popular request, would perform comic songs in his fine tenor.

Every activity was seasoned by a tacit dissidence. To be a Catholic was, among other things, a way of not being a Communist. The study of English was a reaching towards the West at a time when all the governmental pressures were for a reaching towards the East. If you carried it far enough you would understand the BBC news or the disc jockeys on Radio Luxembourg. If you were very lucky, you might get to Britain on a scholarship or exchange trip. Some of the students, as with students anywhere, were idle or cantankerous, but in general there was so much positive energy about that you felt that the individual teacher could make a difference, could help to create an enclave within which people could learn and develop.

Outside this enclave were thickets of stultifying bureaucracy. I'd never before considered the term as implying anything more than a proliferation of paper-work, and there was a lugubrious interest in seeing deeper into the matter. For example, it wasn't the case that decisions were delayed merely by an over-zealous insistence on details of procedure. The procedures themselves were confused and indistinct. Moreover, there were few rewards for speedy arrival at a decision, whereas there could be considerable penalties for making a wrong one. It was natural to procrastinate or pass the buck. When the time came for me to return to England the following summer it took me a whole working day in Lublin to get official permission to leave. Irena Przemecka kindly went to Warsaw one Tuesday in June solely to buy my rail ticket to London, since she thought the transaction might prove complicated. It did: she returned triumphantly with the ticket the following Friday.

Post from England could take anything from four days to a fortnight to arrive. The suspicion was that much of it had been read en route. Facetious friends were liable to include tactless pleasantries – 'spent an agreeable evening with Sir Oswald, who sends greetings' – but no harm seemed to come of it. The newspapers that got through were especially welcome; I came to realise that I'd taken too much for granted the sustenance of hard information and argument about current affairs. How could you think without it? It was true that the ceaseless media propaganda in favour of the government and the Party was reassuringly unpersuasive. Never, either in Lublin itself or in other towns I visited, did I meet a self-confessed Communist, though I did encounter a number of Party-members. Polish news bulletins and governmental pronouncements encountered blunt disbelief. It took me some time to recognise the negative implications of this scepticism. People knew what they disbelieved but not what they did believe. How was it possible, for example, to tell whether the government's housing policy was successful when there was no alternative proposal to weigh it against? If one did have views on such an issue they could be comfortably entertained in the certainty that they would never be put to the test and so perhaps found wanting. Totalitarianism seemed to engender an ideological emptiness or arbitrariness of mind and a strong susceptibility to rumour. I was assured by one professor that the Soviet claim to possess nuclear weapons was mere bluff. Such scientific sophistication was inconceivable, he reasoned, from a nation which couldn't manufacture so much as a functioning electric kettle.

After a few months in Poland I could muster only a little of the political tolerance I'd projected in London. The trite fall-back position in those days was the much-quoted claim that it was impossible to make an omelette without breaking eggs. There were egg-shells galore in Poland in 1959, but the omelette certainly hadn't been served. On the other hand, there were preliminary hints of coagulation, in education, the arts, housing and health. I had sufficient glimpses of a surviving snobbery and anti-Semitism to confirm my sense that pre-War Poland must have been a pretty awful place. How many of the working-class students I was teaching at KUL would have got near a university in those days? How many would have been better clothed or fed? Naturally it was easier to be aware of such considerations if you held a Western passport. Those whose advancement I was con-templating were overwhelmingly likely to see post-War Poland as a dreary tyranny.

The dreariness was certainly inescapable, but it was all in the public sphere. Nothing is more memorable from those days than the contrast between public and private life. Poles gave wonderful parties. Outside, the drab streets, the empty shops; in some particular apartment, colour, music and, somehow, a wonderful spread. Pleasure had been plucked out of the air, as by a conjuring trick. In this area, too, the achievement not only defied the hostile circumstances but seemed to have been engendered by them.

A trip to a Warsaw theatre offered me the aptest image of that year. The curtain was about to rise on *Hamlet* when the building was plunged into darkness by a power cut. The actors appeared on stage with candles to ask whether we would like our money back or would prefer them to carry on as best they could in the circumstances. Carry on, urged the audience. The perform-ance duly went ahead, taking on fresh dramatic life as the cast

Michael Irwin

improvised new groupings and gestures in the small areas of illumination among the deep shadows. Brilliant effects were born of necessity. The ghost appeared in true darkness. Hamlet could hold his candle close to Ophelia's face in an agonized attempt to read her expression. The audience followed the action in rapt sympathy and complicity. It was an anti-climax when the lights eventually came on again and the staging reverted to normal.

Thanks to Professor Mroczkowski his three visiting lecturers spent Christmas in Kraków, where he himself lived – a city relatively unscathed by the war and as yet unpolluted. This was an instructive visit, particularly after three weeks in Lublin. The social environment was different: there seemed to be a lot of former countesses about. We went to a party at Professor Mroczkowski's flat, where his children acted a Christmas play in English and he protruded his head through a book-case to make a guest-appearance as God. Frank Tuohy was there, the British Council lecturer in the newly-opened English Department at the Jagiellonian University. I knew of him already from his novel *The Animal Game* which had grown out of a similar appointment in Brazil. It was through talking to him that I first realised that one might actually be paid reasonably well to travel the world as a teacher.

It was again through Professor Mroczkowski that we were introduced to the new Bishop of Kraków, apparently the youngest bishop in Europe, who had previously taught at KUL. We were told that he had worked in a local factory and acted in an experimental theatre, that he was a keen skier and canoeist. We could see for ourselves that he was handsome, trenchant and benign. When he made to leave, Anne Hargest asked him to give us all a blessing and I had sheepishly to lower a lapsed Catholic knee. That week I wrote to my girlfriend in Scotland to say that I'd met this radical and innovative figure who ought to made Pope – as he would be twenty years on.

Hardly less impressive to me was Claire Dąbrowska, an English woman, married to a Pole, who had lived in Kraków through the War and post-War years and had become central to the University's English Department. She was a phenomenon: through an extraordinary species of self-preservation a pre-War lady in style, manner, cadences and locutions. She was a model of kindness, composure, propriety and dry humour, a touchstone for the new Department. A slight nervous tic gave the impression that she winked now and then at what she herself was saying. It suited her so well that I could never tell where her delicate touches of mockery gave way to the involuntary irony of the wink. It was a demeanour suited to the country.

It was demanding year, if a fascinating one, and I looked forward to getting home. But when I arrived in England that summer I experienced the sense of anti-climax that I have often known since on returning from Poland. Life at home seemed plethoric and underpowered. After completing a postgraduate degree I was glad to get away again, to teach in Japan.

I came back to Poland in the autumn of 1963, this time to take up a British Council lectureship at the state university of Łódź. In the intervening period my longer-term plans had changed and settled. Half a dozen new universities were soon to be established in Britain. To be in at the founding of such an institution seemed an exciting prospect. I'd resolved to teach abroad until I could apply for a post in one of them. Meanwhile I could look for examples of good practice to emulate or bad practice to avoid.

By now the English Department at KUL had indeed been closed down, but its staff – and this was characteristic of Poland – had been neither victimised nor wasted. Some were at the state university in Lublin, Irena Przemecka and Irka Kałuża had joined Professor Mroczkowski in Kraków, while Hała Będrzycka and Irena Janicka, to my great pleasure, were now at Łódź. I found this movement between institutions reassuring after my experience of the Japanese tradition, in which outstanding students stay on at their original university as the acolytes and dependents of an influential professor.

Another group of lecturers, with whom I was to feel particularly comfortable, had come to Łódź from Warsaw University. They'd studied English together in the Stalinist period when every fellow-student of this suspect discipline was a potential informer, and mutual confidence had been hard-won. Vodka had been cheap in those days, they said, and much of the time they'd been drunk. By now, of course, their prospects had been transformed. The Łódź department, headed by Professor Witold Ostrowski[2], seemed to be modestly thriving. I myself was appreciably better off than I'd been in Lublin, with a decent salary from the British Council and nothing much to spend it on. I was married, and after several months at the Łódź Grand Hotel my wife and I were allowed a flying leap over the waiting list and installed in a pleasant flat in a newly-built block not far from the Department. As a Council employee I enjoyed the benefit of duty-free cigarettes and alcohol. It seemed only civil – indeed, a privilege – to dispense these benefits at large. In my recollection Donia and I regularly presided over a sort of whisky-fountain for fellow-lecturers, while we played and replayed the early Beatle LPs and gossiped late into the night.

The academic side of life, however, didn't differ dramatically from that at KUL. There were more books, but not that many more. Constrained by a national syllabus the students had thirty or forty hours of compulsory classes a week, the majority devoted to ancillary subjects such as Russian, Marxism and Economics. There was as much disaffection with the government and its policies as ever there had been at KUL, as much of a sense of being locked into an obtuse and corrupt system that drained energy and wasted talent. I recall the amused bewilderment of Arnold Kettle, who was visiting the Department on a lecture tour, when at a student party he established that he was the only Marxist in the room.

As others have noted, Łódź was a bleak place in those days – an ugly textile town long past its prime. The pavements were muddy and the buildings black. Trams crashed their way along cobbled streets. You would look out of your window even on a fine evening and think: 'Why am I here?' But it had its opera house and its theatres, its university and a film-school that Britain has never remotely emulated. Against reasonable expectations some things were going very well indeed. The English Department, for example, was potentially brilliant, thanks largely to the young lecturers who had converged on it. Some of the students were remarkable: three or four I'd still rank among the most gifted I've taught anywhere.

With hindsight it seems obvious that this was the time when the Department should really have taken off. With the help of influence in the right circles it could have become the centre of university English teaching in Poland. But the moment was allowed to pass. Within a couple of years Jacek Fisiak moved from Łódź to open a new department in Poznań and took a whole team of staff-members and graduate students with him. It was to be the Poznań Department that rapidly grew. A great opportunity had been lost.

I mention this by no means with a view to attaching blame – which in any case wouldn't be an appropriate term. No one outside the system, certainly no one from another country, could begin to guess what were the right personal and political strings to pull, and what might be the moral cost of pulling them. But in broad terms the issue was plain to see: it was a version of a problem visible at every level of a totalitarian society. Any significant institutional achievement entailed cooperating with the authorities. When did such cooperation become collusion? How much did collusion itself matter if the desired end was achieved and some significant general benefit obtained? At either end of the spectrum of possible attitudes there were, it seemed, insidious temptations. A sycophant or charlatan could acquire undeserved power by toeing the Party line and befriending the right people. The result might be (for instance) a well-funded, well-equipped university department of poor academic quality. At the other extreme the responsible professor, incapacitated by integrity, might avoid compromising gestures of any kind and be rewarded with the nothing that comes of nothing. Principles would survive unscathed; meanwhile there would be a loss of potential student places, or library funds, or staff promotions. A university department, like pretty well any other department of Polish life, needed a Schindler in charge to do the compromising, and serve as a moral umbrella for the more fastidious. It's easy enough to be knowingly ironic about such a dilemma from a spectator's viewpoint. In those days it wouldn't have seemed possible that even a shadowy version of such a Hobson's choice could emerge in British university life.

It would be misleading to write about the life of the visiting lecturer in Poland without mentioning how erotic most of us found it. Some years earlier, as we'd heard, a British Council officer named George Bidwell had defected for love of a

Michael Irwin

Polish woman[3]. It was said that he'd written a book about the matter called *I Chose Freedom*. Whenever there was a public statement from a group of writers in support of some measure of censorship or cultural oppression, 'Jerzy Bidwell' would be among the group of toadies who signed it. I genuinely hope that he found his Freedom worth the price he had to pay for it. His predicament was all too imaginable. A number of visiting lecturers – including Anne Hargest and Anita Jones – married Poles. Though I didn't myself, it was a damned close-run thing. A full discussion of this theme might be interesting in its own right, but would certainly prove embarrassing. I mention it in this context only as a particular example of the way in which Polish life under Communism tended to magnify, distort and polarise ideas and emotions of all kinds.

I can't look back on my time in Poland without drawing a variety of morals and inferences. Many of these are personal in application, but some aren't. For example, it's clear to me that the money the British Council spent on its Polish operation was well applied. What more suitable recipients of largesse than those accustomed to make the most of little? The books supplied were eagerly read, the grants and scholarships changed lives. Many of those who were taught in turn became teachers. And many of the visiting teachers, including myself, became so caught up in the place that they went on to foster further contacts of various kinds on their own account.

The environment of post-War Poland dramatised the virtues of idiosyncrasy. The rebuilding of the Old Town in Warsaw has been questioned as well as praised, but apart from its intrinsic aesthetic status it imposed a saving asymmetry on the city. Post-War Warsaw couldn't be reduced to a grid-plan. Comparably, an English department like the one at Kraków that had to accommodate Professor Mroczkowski, autocratic and academically dandiacal, and Claire Dąbrowska, the ladylike epitome of English good sense, couldn't easily be standardised. Although totalitarianism inhibits the influence of individuality, in a less obvious sense it magnifies it.

Not one of my Polish friends of those days but would have looked forward to the end of Communist rule as an impossible dream, an opportunity for transformation. Certainly those from

KUL would have been delighted to learn that the English department there would be reopened. In a number of ways, however, the great transformation has been for the worse. Lecturers must now take second or even third jobs to make ends meet. Departments must divert much of their energy into money-making ventures. Colleagues once united in their opposition to Communist rule may now be bitterly divided by their emerging political allegiances. The West is less generous with help now that the political incentives have dwindled.

But there are ironies on both sides of the ideological looking-glass. When I first gawped at the Palace of Culture, I never dreamed that the ancient buildings of London would soon be dwarfed by scores of sky-scrapers. I assumed then that I was a (very junior) emissary from an assured university tradition. Over the past few years that tradition has been quite casually dismantled, diluted, hacked about. Within the individual university, administrative apparatchiks devise empty Mission Statements and ad hoc Academic Plans in crude managerialese, desperate to propitiate unknown officials. If you've worked in a Communist country you can recognise the hopes and fears and rationalisations at work, but the submission to external pressures seems the more ignominious given the relative feebleness of the threat. In post-War Poland, in the face of real tyranny, the idea of a university was passionately defended, sometimes by outright defiance, sometimes by cunning. What a lot we could learn from that experience.

---

[1] When the hard-line Stalinist period officially came to an end. (ed.)
[2] See his essay 'Stalinism and After' in this book. (ed.)
[3] See also Ibid. and Derwent May for accounts of this event. (ed.)

George Hyde

Don Joins Long March

An abrasive wind from the East; a sense of intellectual oppression growing stronger and stronger; a spreading and pervasive mindlessness; the daily battle with manipulative functionaries and even more manipulative females; hard-nosed Marxist ideologues laying down the law or stabbing one another in the back – these were just some of the compelling reasons for wanting to make a break from Norwich in that memorable long hot summer of 1976, the only time I've ever managed to grow Marmande tomatoes out-of-doors. But this was no ordinary holiday departure. With six trunks packed, a two-year-old in a pushchair and dragging a four-year-old by the hand, we took off not for the South of France, but for the People's Republic of Poland, on a one year contract that turned into three. When people there asked us why we'd come, I used to answer that I'd been trying to get to Russia and had got lost. This was greeted with wary approval and cautious mirth as a plausible allegory; and of course I did, and do, speak Russian, and had written quite a lot about Russian literature, and published translations of some Russian texts, which made it both easier and harder to learn Polish. Paradoxically, perhaps, I had to agree to the British Council striking my Mayakovsky translation from my CV 'in case it caused offence', since the original was written by a Russian Communist.

A cold wind was indeed blowing from the East, and the spectre of Communism still haunted Europe... It wasn't our first time in the new 'people's democracies' that the Russians had established in Central Europe in the wake of Hitler's reign of terror, but this time it was more or less for real: a little flat in a concrete block (rather than the decaying Jugendstil Berliner-zimmer I had been dreaming of); a local food store selling mostly biscuits, bottled fruit and what looked like crushed testicles in jelly; no washing machine, two kids, and not a launderette in town; unsuitable light summer clothes, uncontrollable temper tantrums in the drab but rather decorous Polish street (and the children weren't all that easy to deal with, either); almost irreparable damage to the younger son's pushchair on the BA flight; no sign at all of our six trunks. Could we buy a pair of shoes? but surely Poland exported shoes? you must be able to get shoes somewhere? ah, that was why we couldn't buy a pair of shoes! All sold to the West for hard currency! A piece of sausage, then? ah yes, same difference: all exported, though there were wonderful, heroic stories of railwaymen tying the trains to the tracks, to stop them leaving for the East. A box of matches? slightly easier, in fact no problem at all, provided you didn't mind the Russian sort that either exploded all over your trousers or simply wouldn't strike.

'This country has been devastated,' I announced solemnly to my wife; but it wasn't really true – just that I was beginning to feel that I was not wholly in control, and I was getting a bit apprehensive; and by comparison with Hungary, where we'd recently had a rollicking good holiday, there didn't seem to be much to eat. Only to drink: if you liked vodka. I do. That was something. I soon discovered that vodka was used to slake most cravings. It is the metaphysical booze, bar none. And it soon began to dawn on us – especially after vodka drunk with new, eager friends – that although there was virtually nothing in the shops, what there was was almost free – for us, at least. I made a forlorn, unfunny joke about it: maybe this isn't a free country, but it's almost free. To my surprise, the Poles we were getting to know quite quickly didn't seem to mind jokes like this. Was this a nation of masochists? I asked myself. But the fact was that the best things simply never made it to the shops, which were almost a kind of sideshow. And then someone told us the classic meta-physical-monetarist joke, which ran: average salary 3,000 złotys, average expenditure 6,000 złotys, and you can save the differ-ence. Which everyone seemed to be doing, since it did seem as if there was always cash, even a lot of cash, if people ever needed

George Hyde

it. Evidently the currency was almost as metaphysical as the vodka. People were not obviously going short of things, even if they dressed simply (young women were very stylish) and ate very frugally in between blow-outs and binges (most unconstrained and enjoyable, virtual orgies). Of course, basic services really were very cheap, and this was taken for granted. I started wondering about the women, who were not at all frumpy like Communist women were supposed to be, but unusually pretty and elegant. Were they as metaphysical as the vodka, the currency, and the sausages? I had plenty of time to find out, as it happened.

And everything was so grey! beautifully grey, and silver, and golden, and a dark peeling ochre colour, and without the garish rash of commercialism that has made us so insensitive, in the so-called 'free' world, to the natural colours of nature and things. It was achingly beautiful, quiet, and sad, especially the cemetery in Lublin, a corner of which I still carry in my heart: if I never rest in it, at any rate it will always rest in me! For some reason, no one, Polish or expat, seemed to think much of Lublin as a place, and offered condolences – whereas my wife, who'd just been in Heidelberg, said how much more beautiful Lublin was. Of course, being the William Morris-y sort of Britishers we were, with more than a dash of Arnold and Lawrence, we were delighted by the absence of Eurotrash everywhere. No commercial telly, no big ugly posters, and if half the shops were full of what looked like spares for Soviet vacuum cleaners, well, a lot of people did have Soviet vacuum cleaners, after all, which doubtless needed constant supplies of spares. The necessary splash of colour in the high street was provided by the bookshops – many of them – and the record sleeves in the music shop windows, and flowers, flowers, flowers: I sometimes thought Poles must eat them, or sleep on them, or throw them at one another, they were (and are) so ubiquitous. And the cinemas: to our surprise, they showed lots of Western films. In fact, they showed Hollywood films that had not yet come to Britain, and sometimes in versions the censor had cut less than in Britain; but not only Hollywood films drew huge crowds, in those far-off days. A new Wajda film was always a sensation, as well as being a serious contribution to the dominant political and artistic discourses. When *Man of Marble* was shown, people rose and cheered, especially during the scene where the Stakhanovite hero is fed large slices of ham to build him up! for there was no ham in Poland, or if there was, the workers were the last people to taste it.

No ham? I remember one May Day, when we all marched happily with our banners down the high street, and then went to a restaurant (the Polonia, specialising in national dishes and sexy, folksy waitresses: now closed). There was no vodka (a precaution, because it was a public holiday), only Soviet champagne. No 'proper' meat, only wild boar and venison. And on each table there was a small cut-glass vase with a red carnation. A visiting fellow-traveller would have seen with his own eyes how the Polish worker feasted on game and champers; but what he really wanted, of course, was a slice of ham. It was here that I discovered what everyday life regularly bore out: that there is no one like a Pole for making a virtue out of a necessity, or a bit of theatre out of a commonplace incident. Or, alas, a mountain out of a molehill. In fact, Poland already seemed to me the most semiotic, metaphoric, transformation-scene of a society I had ever encountered outside of the pages of *Alice in Wonderland*. An Alice-in-Wonderland feeling regularly came over foreign visitors: it seemed that a kind of dream logic ruled Poland, rather than the so-called United Worker's Party (Communists), and that the Party had somehow given itself up to the dream as well; so that although you could see Orwellian insignia everywhere in the streets (and in more secret places too) these slogans had, for the most part, become entirely metaphorical, a succession of 'as if' propositions about the deceptiveness of reality. There was a giant conspiracy, maybe at the expense of the Russians. A veil of eroticism and alcohol hung over everything. That same May, the University library building sported a huge placard, or series of placards, reading 'Program partii jest programem': 'the Party's programme is a programme'. It almost looked like an oversight, as if the person responsible had accidentally left off the last, familiar word 'narodu': 'The Party's programme is the programme of the People'. How careless! but of course it wasn't, it was the famous national subversiveness peeping out from the resented institutional context. 'The Party's programme is a programme'. You could buy a t-shirt with 'My nie lubimy ruskich' on

George Hyde

the front ('we don't like Russians') and 'pierożek' on the back – so that the whole innocuously silly message read 'we don't like Russian dumplings' (a staple of Polish cuisine, by the way!) rather than 'Russian soldiers'. You could get involved in quasi-theological debates about the meaning of a slogan like 'Budujemy socjalizm', for instance: 'We are building socialism' or 'Let's build socialism'. Did it matter? What the hell did it mean anyway? There was still a whiff of post-War hysteria and euphoria about, perhaps because the Party assiduously kept the memory of the War alive, for its own purposes. Everyone knew that Poland was probably bankrupt, but they also knew that this put her in some pretty good company, and was not the end of the world: better spend the money we hadn't got as quickly as possible before someone found out! and in this way 'build socialism'.

But life was not all sign-systems, even in Poland. Two children needed looking after, putting to school, dressing, feeding, nursing through colds and worse. Poles were amazed that we were trying to manage without a grandmother (i.e. the one who stood in the meat queues, for there *was* meat, and very good meat, only you had to get up early). Even more amazed that my wife and I would go out of an evening and leave our offspring in the care of a student! paid in food or wine or gramophone records. This was *not* a Polish custom: the Polish family was powerful, inward-looking, and guaranteed one's survival; one could not open it up wantonly to strangers, at least not on our terms (hospitality was quite another matter: it was intense to the point of suffocation, though this has changed recently). The word 'baby-sitter' made people laugh. But the whole apartment block was actually a kind of family: people were in touch, especially when 'the system', as a kind of common enemy, drew them together. If something worth having came into the shops, one of the neighbours would go out of their way to tell us. 'There's cooking oil!' rang round the stairwells. How exciting life became!

And one made friends: very intimate friends, whose lives became woven into one's own, despite the reserve underneath that came from their sense of our privileges, and from the famous Polish Complex. Polish culture has always had a pronounced streak of anarchy, and of masochism; this can be explained in terms of the perennial historical need to subvert some alien authority. So family values (which were themselves seen as subversive of 'the commune') were punctured, or at least punctuated, by wild drinking parties and sexual licence. In the arts, an amazing avant-garde theatre ran to outrageous effects of pure style. Modernism was alive and well. Of course, Poles also took pleasure in leading on the 'cold' and 'naïve' English, thawing them out with drink and sex and game-playing; and if the friendship was real, it could only get stronger and deeper, unbearably so; while if the innate suspicion got the upper hand, out of what Poles refer to among themselves as 'disinterested malice', the whole thing could turn into a gleeful, nasty upstaging of the outsiders. Very complex, and very fascinating, if you didn't get hurt. Many English visitors never recovered. For all of us, life would never be quite the same again. It was hard to explain this to English friends, especially those who had been deluded by Cold War propaganda into thinking that Poland was a depressed vassal state.

Even in academic life, the same combination of traditionalism, drama, and passion ruled. Sometimes it seemed as if the whole objective of education was to humiliate the underdog, who, most of the time, was the student, though academics could subject one another to the same degrading procedures, and the Party was never far away. Polish literature records the phenomenon of the ritual humiliation of the aspiring. We, on the other hand, were fortunate to have a remarkable Head of Department, now dead, who was able to make a particularly anarchic (and gifted) bunch of people pay close attention to problems that needed to be solved in the long term, while still acting as a sort of father-figure, as he did to us too as a family. The Party's presence was accepted with a nod and a wink, and no one got too upset. Students summoned from seminars to report to the police on what I had been saying and doing (and I was young enough at the time to invite them to big drunken parties, which were certainly infiltrated by informers) then reported back to me. Students who visited me in England once were asked the strangest question by the police, which translated goes something like: 'Is their house in Norwich as big a tip as their flat in Lublin?' – as well as the predictable, 'And what books does Dr Hyde have on his shelves?' (hoping with ritualistic fervour for the answer 'Solzhenitsyn'!) My little £50 heat-copier, terribly inefficient as it was, was confiscated by the Lublin police, then transferred to the Institute office: they were afraid I was going to distribute copies of *The Gulag Archipelago*; but I had it at home in the end. There were no photocopiers except the one in the main library, closely guarded.

Underneath this vexed surface some organic ties were forming that have never been severed. Poland was, and is, always interesting; we all learned the language, more or less well, and my elder son would interpret for us if necessary. Teaching made both of us many friends, and many of them are still close to us. There was the student whose parents had a small but very efficient farm (he came one day with sausages; 'They are made from my mother', he announced proudly; and one day a pike he had caught was still lively enough to bite my son). Another student couple (with whom we fell in love) introduced us to artists, took us to some fantastic theatre, accompanied us on trips to the incredibly remote, wild-seeming Polish countryside, with all its myths and monsters still intact, lovingly nurtured by a generation which was determined at all costs to resist Communist conformism and had not yet encountered the more insidious blandishments of capitalism. The arts fed voraciously off the permanent sense of stress, striving to articulate the unsayable, to hold up a distorting mirror to a distorted reality. Cultural life was handsomely funded by the State, which was repaid in surreal and subversive forms that kept the avant-garde alive longer than anywhere else in Europe, not just as a trend but almost as if it was the bread-and-butter of the culture. Teaching Modernism and Lawrence (especially), I felt as if I was still living in their heyday and that my favourite academic literary issues were those of the world outside my window. It was a pretty good place for us would-be intellectuals: Communism had stopped the clock. What a paradox this was for the movement that promised to usher in humanity's rational future! Never was there anything less uniform once you scratched the surface; never was thought freer or more anarchic. Of course, a lot of people were playing the system, while cultivating their gardens elsewhere. Others were persecuted, or languished in jail. But as someone said to me, if you didn't put your head up over the parapet, it was a good life.

It certainly was nothing like as degrading as Western propaganda kept telling us, even if you did need a break from it now and then. But then, we Brits represented the *détente* policy which paid off so handsomely in the end.

To tell the truth, it took nearly all of us (Poles and English) by surprise when Solidarity happened. We'd got so used to saying one thing and doing another, swapping English lessons for cognac and sausage, striking out to the incredibly cheap holiday houses in the woods or by the sea when we needed a rest, queuing interminably, it seemed, for marvellous quasi-clandestine theatre that seemed to come bubbling up from some volcanic fissure at the heart of society. Of course, Solidarity meant that under all the self-divisions of this very complex self-dramatising society there really was some sort of consensus, and that the accumulated resentment against the deprivations, the propaganda, and the intermittent threatening gestures, had spoken out in a united voice, the voice of 'the people' as opposed to the manufactured rhetoric of the proletariat. Yet even at the time it seemed odd that 'the people' had taken their lead from a trade unionist working in a shipyard that was only kept open by massive government subsidies; because every aspect of life in People's Poland reflected, in its way, the dominant ideology. That was what had kept the jokes so pointed, the ironies so keen, the 'alternative' art so mainstream. England seemed such a snug little island when one came home for vacations – and so dull, after a few weeks. And people were so ill-informed about Poland, and mostly so uninterested, as if it didn't matter. And perhaps they were right, it didn't; so that although Solidarity and martial law attracted the attention of millions, when these crises passed, and Poland took its 'rightful' place again at the end of the queue of European nations, and Communism's spectre was once again laid (for the time being) to rest, and everyone started wondering how the Cold War had ever come about in the first place, and why we had taken this socialist paper tiger for the real beast, the effect in Poland herself, no longer martyred to Russian imperialism, was not what one had expected at all.

For two years or so, Eastern Europe was the sexiest place in the world. Students back at UEA, Norwich, signed up in droves for my seminar called 'Reading Eastern Europe', then took off for the East with their haversacks and ten dollars a day. Then something started to change: gradually at first, then with gathering momentum. I observed it mainly from a distance, having settled back home, got promoted, published a lot more (including some work on Polish literature, which attracted quite a bit of attention). The Polish consumerist 'revolution' seemed to be running out of steam. Something was not working out as it should, in the deliverance of Poland and other Eastern European countries from the Communist yoke. Should I go back and take another look? Would the Council appoint me again, sixteen years on, now that they, too, had become notoriously managerial, triumphantly convinced that the West Knew Best?

George Hyde's piece on his year in Kraków (1992-93) can be found on p. 125.

Jessica Munns

The Good Old
Bad Old Days

In 1977 I got a British Council job teaching English Literature at the Wysza Szkoła Pedagogiczna in Bydgoszcz. At that time, Poland did not mean much more to me than Chopin and concentration camps. Beyond that, Poland was swathed in the mystification of the Cold War era, an Iron Curtain Country, a place of commissars and secret police, repression, danger and all the sinister romance of John Le Carré novels.

My expectations of romance and danger were fully met at my first British Council briefing. A suitably thin and grey man from the Foreign Office informed me and the other recruits that as soon as our names had been forwarded to the Polish Ministry of Higher Education, a secret file would be opened on us. Once in Poland, our every move would be watched and noted. Quite probably our apartments and telephones would be bugged and there would be police informers amongst our colleagues and students. We were warned to be at all times discreet, to avoid political discussions, and never ever to hand out any political or religious materials. We must break absolutely no laws, even parking laws, and never ever change money on the Black Market. The 'watchers' and 'informers' would note all such activities and at any time when political conditions altered for the worse and Poland wished to rebuke England we would be arrested, deported and generally cause trouble and embarrassment to Her Majesty's Government, whose representatives we were.

It had never been an aim of mine to be a model representative of HMG either at home or abroad, and I had considerable contempt for Cold War propaganda projecting Communist bloc countries as places of deprivation and grim horror. Nevertheless, it was tremendously exciting to imagine oneself a constant object of interest to men in trench coats, not to mention teaching Chaucer or George Eliot to students, some of whom would be doubtless listening carefully as they scanned one's words for political subversion.

I arrived in Warsaw on a cold rainy day in September and was put on the train for Bydgoszcz. The train was all that a central European train should be: slow, ancient and stately with wide carriages, wonderfully ornate lamp-shades and black tea served in glasses in the 'Wars' restaurant car, which itself looked like a set for *Murder on the Orient Express*. Trundling past roads with horse-drawn carts and through a level landscape of thick forests and long narrow strips of fields on which I could see horses drawing wooden ploughs, I seemed to be travelling into the past – into a Breughel landscape rather than into the heart-land of the Warsaw Pact nations.

At Bydgoszcz, I returned to the present as I and my bags were stuffed into a tiny Fiat and dashed round to a modern apartment block where a party in my honour was well under way. There were elaborate and delicious sandwiches, vast quantities of drink, very loud Western pop music, and modern and elegant furniture. All my new colleagues spoke incredibly fluent and colloquial English, seemed to have travelled all over Britain and Europe, and were much more fashionably dressed than I was (be safe I had thought, wear tweeds). As in most Polish universities, most of the Humanities faculty were women, and they told me of their great disappointment at the British Council sending them another woman. They then kindly cheered me up by telling me how attractive Polish men found Western women (even those who came in tweeds, they implied). They were also immediately outspoken about their undoubtedly subversive political views as well as eager to change money at attractive Black Market rates. It was obviously a dreadful plot to get me immediately deported back to England. Or, perhaps, it was just the way things were.

During the next few months I settled into life in Poland with what seemed to me, at least, incredible ease. Indeed, I stayed in Poland for six years, moving from Bydgoszcz to Lublin in 1979. I was not always happy but I was rarely bored. What was more in evidence than either an ideally progressive or evilly repressive society was a lifestyle much more socially and geographically static than in England, much more family oriented, and deeply religious. Families appeared to have lived in the same district, town, even house, for generations, and they all knew each other or of each other. A town official might be a powerful Party figure, but he was also a man who had been to school with one's mother, whose father used to sell wood on the Black Market during the War, whose daughter was on drugs, whose sister married a man from Łódź but returned two years ago without him, whose uncle was a priest and whose aunt lived on a farm and made great sausages.

I shall never know if any of my students or colleagues were 'spying' on me. Occasionally, someone would take me aside and inform me that this or that faculty member or student was a 'spy', but it was never clear if this confidence was passing malice, a moment of sensationalism or the truth. Some members of the departments I worked in were Party members but were usually at pains to make it clear that their membership was a mere formality. There was a sort of double bluff going on all the time: everyone was supposed to be pro-Party but also equally anxious to let it be known that they were really not at all pro-Party, with the result that one never really knew who really was or really was not. Only one of my Polish friends ever told me that she had been summoned to the milicja and asked about the foreigners in the department; possibly more had been but they kept it to themselves. For a little while, I dated a man whom various people told me was probably a police spy. I doubted this, and anyway I found it very erotic to imagine that he was compelled to make love to me. I liked to imagine him dashing off to report on our encounters, 'Yes, Comrade Commissar, I have significant information, she likes to have her ears nibbled.'

The belief that one is being surveyed is, of course, as effective as any real surveillance: it seeps into all relationships. The voyeuristic mixture of uncertainty, anxiety and excitement produced by the idea of secret surveillance functions as an erotic

Jessica Munns

system, an extension into the public sphere of all our private doubts about and probings of each other – where were you when I phoned? who were you talking to at the bar? who are the people in that photograph? It could obsess people – foreigners and Poles alike. From time to time there would be outbreaks of anxiety, with friends putting hair or thin threads across their doors to see if anyone entered while they were out or dodging in and out of doorways convinced they were being followed. At times we would all be caught up in a Voice of America wave of paranoia, and life would seem rather like being in a gritty Cold War movie. Most of the time, however, life just seemed gritty, a daily round of struggling onto over-crowded trams, remembering never to leave the house without a shopping-bag in case one found a shop selling something one wanted and queuing up in Pewex shops for tea and coffee.

My students at both Bydgoszcz and Lublin were delightful. They had wonderful names like Kazimierz, Stanisław, Małgorzata, Bogmiła and Mirosława and usually even longer diminutives which they begged me to use. My Bydgoszcz students helped me enormously, taking me round the town, showing me how to shop, and teaching me useful everyday Polish. They were much more polite than English students and much more respectful. The girls tended to curtsey when they met one, the boys to bow, but although my students at first seemed even overly polite – which made it difficult to start up a discussion in class as everyone civilly agreed with whatever I said – they were not without a leavening of malice and wit. For example, on the first occasion that I needed to buy a ticket to go to Warsaw, various members of my class carefully taught me what I needed to say but also added a request for large quantities of alcohol, until eventually one of the class took pity on me. My students were not only fun and good-hearted but they spoke remarkably good English, endured an incredible number of hours of classes on a wide range of subjects from military service to Marxism to large doses of linguistics, and like everyone else they were quite fearlessly outspoken on political issues. They were scornful of their government, usually ardently Roman Catholic, and keen to take me to cafés and bars where I could listen to anti-government songs or to the theatre to watch plays which they eagerly explained were intensely and critically political and deeply anti-Russian.

They lived in a society which critically evaluated all pieces of information, and in literary criticism classes there was never any need to explain that what is absent from the text may be more significant than what is present. They were deconstructing representations in their cradles. One day after I had returned from a visit to Kraków, I asked my class if there had been anything in the news about the city, since shortly after my train left the station, it was stopped and milicja with dogs rushed on board and searched every compartment. One student produced a newspaper and read through it intently before suddenly crowing with laughter. On the back page, in small print, there were a few sentences announcing that the statue of Lenin in Nowa Huta was in excellent condition. Clearly, the student pointed out, it had been defaced in some way and the police were still searching for the perpetrators.

The power of particular interpretations of the past to create a sense of national identity in terms of struggles against invaders and oppressors was omnipresent. Nearly every month it seemed there was some special day commemorating an event from Poland's past, which students and faculty would mark by wearing some special article of clothing or adornment – a dark pullover, or a particular flower in the lapel – all of which would signify solidarity with some quintessentially Polish historical event, usually a defeat. People would speak bitterly of the 18th century partition of Poland as if it had occurred within their memory, or refer to battles against the Teutonic knights rather as my English contemporaries might recall World War II battles – events belonging to the past but still alive in the collective national memory. The Second World War was vitally present not only to the generations who had lived through it but to those who had not. Poles of all ages would greet me warmly and tell me that they continued to like the English despite England's double betrayal of Poland, first in failing to send the British fleet and army to save Poland from the German invasion and second in selling out Poland to Russia at Yalta.

A profound sense of cultural superiority – of their own elegance, style and grace, and of their deep connection to

Jessica Munns

Western Europe through history, music and literature – gave many of the people I met a strong sense of Russian influence and of Communism as a brief and tasteless episode in their checkered but clearly glorious history. At a reception I once went to in Warsaw given by some minister from the Ministry of Higher Education, I was introduced by the minister to his mother, a very chic old lady dressed in lace and satin and sitting rather as on a throne in an antique armchair. She spoke no English and my Polish was still pitiful, but like many of her generation she spoke French. When she learnt where I was working she expressed great horror: 'Ah comme c'est terrible, Bydgoszcz, mon dieu, c'est une ville plein des Russes et des communistes.' I looked to see what the Minister made of this denunciation of the great ally and the Party, but as far as I could see he was nodding in polite agreement while I, ever aware of the F.O. warnings, burbled on about lovely old buildings and beautiful forests before being dismissed. The most usual reaction of the Poles I met to the Russian presence was that of lofty scorn for the powerful but dumb, 'niekulturalny' – uncultivated – Russians. A Polish joke: Brezhnev is being taken around Warsaw by Gierek. Many of the streets and squares have religious names, but as he whisks Brezhnev around the city, Gierek busily makes up good Party names: Lenin Square, he announces, Socialist Way, Workers' Walk, etc. Then they stop at a traffic light and Brezhnev can see a big street sign saying Our Saviour. 'Is that the square of Our Saviour?' he asks. Gierek nods miserably. 'Ah,' says Brezhnev puffing out his chest with pride, 'what flatterers you Poles are.'

Communism, in many ways, never really seemed to have a chance to gain national consensus, or even to seek it. I could never understand how or why a government which had control of most of the means of communication managed to fail so miserably in the realm of propaganda. The official, unconvincing and dreary representations of socialist internationalism and Party nationalism would take the form of horrifically long speeches by Party officials at graduation exercises. On May Day and October Revolution Day, rather quaintly old-fashioned posters would appear depicting Lenin, beard jutting forward heroically, patting the heads of children of many races. In villages there were always faded banners declaring that the Party's will was the people's will, or extolling the joy of working for socialism and Poland. Long speeches about Polish industrial production contrasted very strongly with the thrill of sitting in cafés singing 'forbidden' songs, and old-fashioned political posters could not possibly compete with avant-garde political theatre. In the countryside, the villages perked up incredibly when their toilet-roll strips of cloth announcing the virtues of labour were effaced by the banners and pictures, ribbons and flowers that were strung up when a copy of the Black Madonna was making its rounds.

Catholicism was, in fact, more pervasive than Communism. Socialism was, as it were, taken for granted: free schooling, free medicine, cheap housing, free or heavily subsidized seaside and spa hotels owned by one's factory or institution, three year long maternity leave with full benefits and job security, were assumed as natural, and, therefore, criticized. In contrast to the assumed infrastructure, innovation always lay elsewhere. The only new buildings going up seemed to be churches. Built or half-built, they were crammed to overflowing with people, with loudspeakers outside the doors relaying the service for the crowds gathered on the pavement. The seasons of the year were religious seasons. In autumn, banners would pronounce the October Revolution, but the real event was All Souls' Eve with the graveyards suddenly turning into surreal and beautiful groves filled with flowers and glowing at night with hundreds of candles. Winter was Christmas, carp swimming in the bath, the streets filled with families going to midnight mass. At Easter, beautifully dressed children would troop to church with baskets filled with eggs, salt, sugar and other goodies to have them blessed, and in summer there were the pilgrimages and the festive trips taken by blessed copies of the Black Madonna.

Everyone lived between these two great systems, taking the bits they wanted from both. My friends would get married in church but unhesitatingly get a civil divorce if they changed their minds or pop to the doctor to abort an unwanted pregnancy. Despite a fierce Church campaign, contraception was widely practiced, which was a good thing, as pre- and extra-marital sex were also widely practiced. Both State and Church had their mechanisms of forgiveness; Poles who had failed to return from visits abroad but now wanted to return would make donations to a State institution; and then there was always confession. One All Souls' Eve, my then boyfriend (not the 'spy') arrived unexpectedly at my flat, hurled himself on top of me and we made passionate love in the hallway. Gosh, I thought, my head wedged beneath the hat-stand, I must be irresistible tonight. Equally rapidly, he leapt to his feet and dashed to the door, and as I asked where the hell he thought he was going, he looked shocked and pointed out it was All Souls and now he must hurry to confession before taking communion at mass. One lived in a world of endlessly proliferating rules and regulations issuing from Church and State, nearly all of which were regularly broken and, indeed, many of which had to be broken if one was to survive.

Alongside these two 'systems,' there ran a third: the Black Market economy which produced a sort of Black Market mentality. There were networks of 'friends' constantly exchanging favours and some people, men in particular, would gain social status from their reputation as wonderful fixers, people one went to whenever one wanted to get something done. There was, in fact, a sense of horror, even scandal, about doing things officially and simply. At one time the battery of my car died and no amount of hauling it up to the flat for recharging over night could resuscitate it. When my friends learnt I had been so simple-minded as to go to the local state garage and order a new one, they were deeply shocked. Instead, a wonderful scheme was evolved whereby I would borrow a friend's battery, and another friend who had an aunt across the Soviet border in Lwów, where batteries were apparently available, would then get a visa to visit a relative, drive my car there, purchase a battery via his aunt with my dollars, conceal the existing battery and return. Petrol for the journey, also in short supply, would be supplied by the uncle of yet another friend who worked on the railways and had access to their petrol stores. In vain I protested that the garage had said they would get me one and that if they did not, I could probably order one from West Germany. The cost of it all, they moaned, the thousands of złotys I would be paying the garage, even worse, the dollars I would pay the West Germans, just a little bit of planning and about $20, and I'd have a fine Russian battery; Jurek or Janek would see his aunt who adored him;

Paweł's or Kazimierz's uncle would get some dollars which he needed to buy bathroom fittings from Pewex for the house he was building, and the car could be stocked with that red Georgian champagne I liked so much. It was a superb plan. Happily, the garage came up with a new battery before all the stages of it were fully worked out. Life often seemed strained, but also vital and intense and not a little schizophrenic.

When it all got too much for me, I would make one of my book and food trips up to the British Council in Warsaw. The British Council in Jerozolimskie Street was a reassuring place. In its own way it was every bit as quaint and old-fashioned as Lenin's beard. The walls were hung with suitably unexciting pictures of the royal family, or those Constablesque vistas of the English landscape that immediately provoke a sort of quiet, grim nostalgia for school. The loo-paper, which was of the hard shiny variety, said 'Strictly Property of her Majesty's Government', so one felt both abused and privileged to use it; the library was full of English books, magazines and newspapers, and when one went to the British Embassy club – 'the Pink' – for lunch there were things like fish fingers and baked beans on toast on the menu. I would shop at the embassy where I could buy luxuries like marmite, marmalade, Heinz tomato soup, very cheap tax and duty-free booze, and quite incredibly, since the one thing that was always available in the shops was a wonderful variety of freshly baked breads, wrapped loaves of English white-sliced bread.

I often stayed overnight at the homes of British Council officials, homes filled with English furniture, tables serving English food, and seemingly totally insulated from the world outside. I would not have wanted to live like that in Poland, but it was tremendously pleasant to spend the occasional weekend wrapped in a sort of cocoon of Britishness, comfortably exchanging jokes about Poland and listening to the latest stories of idiocies perpetrated by other embassies. There was a sort of guilty pleasure to it as I 'betrayed' my Polish life by laughing at it and pretended to myself that I was part of this carefully constructed and comfortable world of Britishness, Cooper's Oxford marmalade, pink gin, bridge parties, and children at boarding school.

Jessica Munns

In this cosy milieu, I discovered colonial attitudes which I had thought to be a feature of pre-War novels about life in rubber-plantations. This time the attitudes were of the colonizers, not the colonized; not scorn for the crude and arrogant oppressor, but rather that effortless and even kindly superiority that comes when one lives close to a people but not with them, and when one is materially, at least, much richer than those people. Each group, the Poles with regard to the Russians, the British with regard to the Poles, and probably in their lonely barracks the Russians with regard to both groups, were engaged in that process whereby their own sense of identity was maintained by 'othering' another group marked out by culturally agreed signs of inferiority. I once heard of a BBC interview with Dame Freya Stark in which she was asked if she thought travel broadened the mind and, after a very long and ruminative pause, she replied 'no.' She made sense.

Shopping was the great trial and adventure of life in Poland. Often when I got to the Department, someone would rush in to say that lemons, or paper handkerchiefs were on sale at a shop on the other side of town and everyone would consult their time-tables to work out who could go and queue up for us all. Like everyone else, I spent a lot of my time in food queues, propped up against a wall reading a book, stopping off now and then to agree with my fellow queuers that I was not Polish and this was boring. When I moved to the Marie Curie University in Lublin, shopping improved as there was a big peasants' market where one could buy eggs and vegetables and even meat, dead or alive, and if one had a taste for it, though I never did, bottles of duck's blood.

Despite, or perhaps because of the shortages, people entertained lavishly and with immense pride. Going to dinner always seemed rather like the transformation scene at a pantomime. I'd be invited into a small flat and then before my eyes it would alter to a first class restaurant. A table would unfold, a linen tablecloth would be whisked out from a suitcase under the sofa-bed, cutlery and glasses would appear and then dish after dish of fish *en gelée*, bowls of barszcz with twisted puff pastry sticks, bigos, pierogi, sliced ham, fresh and picked vegetables, bottled fruits, cakes, tarts and bottles and bottles of flavoured vodkas. Not to eat massively was taken as an insult – and since I hate to be rude, I obliged. Not to drink deeply was similarly deplored, and how could one refuse to drink to Poland, to our hostess, to long life, at least a hundred years, to Poland again, to our hostess' mother whose pig we were eating – the list of toasts was ingenious and endless... Thus I regularly returned home picking my way with inebriated care across ruts in the snow humming the Polish drinking song, 'Sto Lat' ('May You Live to be a Hundred'), and wondering how I'd teach the next day.

Life changed once Solidarity emerged from the underground to the foreground. The most palpable change was the increase in shortages due to the constant strikes and hoarding – though people also spoke darkly of vast heavily guarded storehouses, filled to bursting with commodities which were being witheld from circulation. There was a new strange sort of art-work in the shops where there was very little to buy but the assistants had nonetheless beautifully arranged things like bottles of pickled cucumbers in little pyramids. Following my mother's death, my father had joined me in Lublin and proved to be an incredible asset in those hard times. Not only did he remember various English wartime recipes for cooking nourishing meals out of two turnips and a dried egg, but he became a local pet. Apparently the sight of a shambling elderly Englishman dressed in disreputable cord trousers and a patched jacket and mumbling incredibly mispronounced Polish brought out the patriotic mother in shop assistants. They would dart out from behind counters and secretively but tenderly thrust a wrapped package into his wire basket and, while he protested that he wanted no privileges, they would push him firmly towards the check-out. When he arrived home, we would unwrap these packages and find amazing treats such as cheese, a piece of ham, or a stick of sausage.

The alternative economy networks now really came into play, and produced marvellous acts of generosity. When my next-door neighbours came back with two dozen eggs after scouring the countryside, they insisted on giving us a dozen. Neighbours I hardly knew would knock on the door and deposit a canteen of soup. And the dinner parties... We would gather at each other's houses with our various offerings – mine were usually bought at

Pewex – and eat incredible and strange meals while everyone talked excitedly about the 'thaw', about Lech Wałęsa, about being on strike, about rumours of Russian troops hiding in the forests, about East German troops on maneuvers at Frankfurt-an-der-Oder, about Wajda's latest film. There was a tremendous feeling of hope and excitement. I remember a friend sitting in a café excitedly waving a newspaper at me and saying, 'Look at me, look at this, two months ago this would be samizdat, the author would be in jail, I'd be afraid to read it in public, now it's just *Trybuna Ludu's* lead article.'

There were also sinister signs and movements – right-wing patriotic groups could now 'register' as unions – and the strain of anti-Semitism which one often sensed not far beneath the cultural surface reappeared as people told each other anti-Semitic jokes about the national government spokesman, who was said to be a Jew. In an outbreak of overt anti-Semitism, the actor boyfriend of a Jewish friend of mine was asked to either give up his girlfriend or leave the company. Fearing this was only the start, they took advantage of the easing up of travel restrictions and both left the country. The phrase which Wałęsa made popular, 'Poles speaking to Poles', was widely quoted and in an ethos of renewed and vigorous patriotism and Catholic nationalism could sound ominous. The Church was very active, and a busy day at the striking University would begin with prayers and hymns. Solidarity was fast becoming everything: a trade union negotiating better conditions and pay increases, and at one nearby striking factory, demanding pay in dollars and colour TVs for all employees. It was also a reassertion of nation and faith, as well as a political party demanding every sort of reform, human rights, political rights, women's rights, clean air, uncensored news media, free elections, freedom of travel, and the expulsion of Russian troops. Everyone saw whatever they wanted through the lens of Solidarity, which was to deliver everything, West German wealth and old Polish morals, advanced liberties and traditional rights.

On December 13, 1981, the day martial law was declared, I had 'flu and stayed at home feeling sorry for myself and therefore missed the tanks rolling into town. Suddenly around four in the afternoon friends rushed in asking if we were alright, and had the troops bothered us? Poking my head out of front door, I discovered that the block was indeed surrounded by armored personal carriers, troops and a tank. We all gathered around the TV and watched as fat men in rather stiff uniforms made speeches and the usual announcers, also in rather uncomfortable uniforms, listed all the things we could not do and announced the hours of the curfew. More friends arrived. There was no transport and so they had walked across town to check that we were safe. We ate, we drank, we all wept a bit, we got drunk. One of my friends was an Argentinean journalist and a specialist in military coups. We were all a little numb and aghast, but he would wave at the TV and say things like, 'Now just you see, they have no more to say for a little, so they will play us military music and show us tanks, then a few battleships, soon a fly over by fighters, this is essential, we must see that all the military are united.' He was quite right, and the moment the little fat men left, tanks appeared on the screen to the sounds of rousing military music. It all began to seem terribly absurd and funny, not strange after all but hilariously predictable. We rolled help-lessly on the sofa calling for battleships and jets, and battleships and jets duly appeared.

The University was closed; the Rektor was arrested. No one knew what was happening anywhere else. There were no telephones, no transport, and no news except the listing of the rules and the tanks and jets. After a few days the Rektor was let out on parole and when I went to see him, he urged me to leave Poland. Everyone urged us to leave, taking lists of the names of the arrested to England and messages to relatives in England letting them know their families were safe. Leaving, however, felt horrible, and in any case was not so simple with no petrol for the car, no trains, no buses, no knowledge of what was happening in other towns. The World Service of the BBC, which we listened to intently, could not help much since the journalists were in the same position, trapped in Warsaw. At least, however, we knew that there was no fighting going on in Warsaw, just endless rumours of barricaded factories, miners refusing to leave the pits, stories of soldiers either firing or refusing to fire on strikers. People had believed in the Army, which was seen as a patriotic army, an army which had once defeated the Russians, a regular army, people said, made up of their sons and brothers, which would never really fire on Poles. In Lublin, people had also believed in Jaruzelski, who came from a old Lubelski gentry Army family. As much as anything else, I believe people were in shock at seeing their army station its tanks and APCs around their homes, their schools and universities and their hospitals and factories.

After a few days, train services to Warsaw resumed and various categories of people, including foreigners and the elderly, could travel, and my father and I made the journey to Warsaw, not without numerous emotional farewells. When we arrived at the British Council we had a heroes' welcome. We were their first lambkins up from the provinces. We were rushed over to the Embassy in a splendid car with CD plates, passing through peopleless streets, across processions of tanks and over check-points guarded by heavily armed soldiers in long overcoats hud-dled around braziers. The embassy ballroom, usually at this time of the year swathed in streamers for the Christmas Fayre, was Operations HQ with trim girls perched on stools behind monitor screens, telephones, and people scurrying to and fro looking happy and excited. Then the military attaché appeared – dressed to perfection. Jodhpurs and boots struck a strong military note with reassuring colonial overtones on his lower half, and a Norfolk jacket, open shirt and cravat struck an untroubled country gentleman note on his upper half. I felt so terribly proud of being British. Ah well, I thought, we may not be a great power any longer, but whatever the occasion, invasions, coups or sherry parties, we do know how to dress.

Quite rapidly, the universities were reopened and I returned as fast as I could. No one in my department had been arrested. We were all more or less as we had been. Rationing had vastly improved the food situation and the curfew had been extended a bit. Quite soon telephones were restored, now with a voice which came on to tell one that all calls were being monitored, which produced a new batch of stories about monitors interrupting conversations to say that was no way to talk to a lady or informing the speaker that the girl he had just spoken to had made a date with another man not five minutes ago. Maybe it was my imagination, but I recall a feeling of shame and embarrassment. There had been such confidence, such a feeling that Solidarity was invincible, that the Army was really pro-Solidarity too, that no Pole would oppress another Pole, and now in one night, in one brief series of movements by the armed forces, it was all over.

There were soldiers everywhere, heavily armed and in groups, in little squads, never less than three. This produced another joke, or the recycling of an old one: 'Why do they always go about in threes? One to read, and one to write, and one to watch over these dangerous intellectuals.' We all lived through those immediate post-Solidarity, martial law months, as I recall it, in a great national depression occasionally lifted by daft jokes and acts of courage. Once I saw a young Polish woman, dressed as Polish women often are, with enormous elegance in a fur-trimmed coat and fur hat, walk with serene and undeviating grace across the Old City square in Warsaw. The serenity and the lack of deviation in her route were remarkable because directly in her way as she walked was a small squad of soldiers, packs of three and three also moving across the square and holding their machine guns in front of them, a habit I always found quite unnerving. My serene walker, however, appeared not to notice them, not to see them, and it was they who deviated, made way, stepped out of her path before she cannoned into them and not even this movement was acknowledged – every line of her body indicated complete indifference, the soldiers simply did not exist because they should not exist.

I left Poland two years later, but not before Pope Jan Pawel II's first visit inaugurated a new wave of optimism, and not before, much to my embarrassment, my university presented me with a huge bouquet of orchids to mark Britain's recapture of the Malvinas Islands. In December '81, it seemed the 'odwac', the thaw, was to be followed by a long winter of repression; instead, first gradually and then rapidly, a new, different, maybe better society emerged. Now I chatter on e-mail to my friends at the university in Lublin about films we have all seen and books we have all read – and annoy them with nostalgia for the good old bad old days of anxiety, sharing, cheating and heroism.

Gary Mead

'Happy Days'

Inow feel that my life only really started when, at the age of 25, I went to Poland in September 1979, to live and work in one of the most depressing towns imaginable, even by Communist East European standards. I went to Bydgoszcz, pronounced something like 'Bidgosh'. It was an unlovely place in those days, its buildings crumbling, facades collapsing, a smell of stale beer, acrid tobacco and ancient vegetables lingering in every greasy shop doorway and office. The prominent feature of the city's main square – next to the old quarter – was an eternal flame, constantly burning in memory of Poles executed by the invading Germans in the Second World War. A hundred yards away was the tawdry glitter of the local Pewex shop, where for hard currency, not Polish złotys, you could buy western chocolate, cigarettes, perfumes, even condoms and intra-uterine devices.

I cannot say what Bydgoszcz may now be like. Though I have once been back to Warsaw, in February 1993, I have never returned to the city where I spent almost four years of my life. I left Bydgoszcz in July 1983, a casualty – with partially self-inflicted wounds – of the military rule imposed on December 12 1981 by the military-Communist régime of General Wojciech Jaruzelski.

In late spring 1979 I was running out of taxpayers' money. Living in Oxford, that most seductively enervating of intellectual and social hothouses, I was finishing a one-year post-graduate teacher-training course, but was desperately trying to avoid actually landing up as a secondary school teacher. Things were not going as I had planned. In 1975 I had gained a first class degree in Philosophy and English at Newcastle University. I stayed on there to do a doctorate with vastly ambitious scope, but I had a very instrumental attitude towards the research; I was doing it to get an academic job, not because of its intrinsic interest. It was bound to end badly.

I drifted to Oxford from Newcastle. By 1979 the doors of British universities were thudding shut against all those would-be academics without a completed Ph.D. The more apparent it became I would not get an academic post without finishing the thesis, the more impossible it became to sit down and write. It's a familiar problem.

Fate has always intervened at crucial moments, steering me not with a gentle hand in the small of the back but a large boot in the rear. At the end of my teacher-training I was made an offer difficult to refuse but easy to dislike: a teaching post at what was then the largest comprehensive school in England, in the heart of Milton Keynes, whose very name is, for me, synonymous with being buried alive. The interviewing panel would not allow me more than 15 minutes' stroll in the school playground to consider my reply. Enough time to toss a coin to make the decision. A miraculous escape; I turned it down.

The following week a stranger telephoned me in Oxford. It was a British Council officer. She told me I had failed to get the job of Senior Lecturer in English Literature at Lublin University, Poland, for which I had recently been interviewed. But there was suddenly a post available at Bydgoszcz, a place which the caller couldn't pronounce. I had no idea where it was, save in Poland. The salary on offer, at fractionally more than £2,000 per annum, was a quarter of that for the Lublin job. Poor, even by the rotten standards of teaching; and again I had to make up my mind immediately.

This time I tossed no coin. I went to Poland. Almost four years later I was arrested, my Council contract terminated; and I returned to England without a job. But the wheel of fate continually turns. It now seems quite natural that the black sheep of 1983 is, a decade and a half later, writing a brief memoir of his sheepish blackness in the company of several other erstwhile employees of the very same institution which once could not get rid of him quickly enough.

Gary Mead

In early May 1983, at about three in the afternoon, I was heading for bed – a narrow uncomfortable couch with a thin foam mattress on top – with a cheese sandwich, a bottle of local Bydgoszcz beer, and the latest Ed McBain novel. That was a pretty normal procedure. From my first year in Poland I had got into a routine – thanks to a lengthy bout of insomnia – of crashing out in the afternoon and early evening, and of working or socialising late into the night. My teaching load was undemanding, about ten contact hours a week, plus preparation and marking.

This particular day had been fairly disastrous. I had tried showing a film of *Under Milk Wood* to some students but towards the end of the movie the Bulgarian-manufactured projector went into meltdown, fusing the last few feet of the film into a black mess. How was I going to explain that to the Council in Warsaw?

I never had to; I was instead saved by a three-day stint in the local Bydgoszcz milicja HQ, charged with 'defaming the Polish Peoples' Republic in the foreign mass media', an offence carrying a jail term of one-to-ten years.

I had just bitten into the sandwich – the cheese was an ubiquitous type called 'salami', which Poles said compensated for never being able to buy genuine salami – when the doorbell of my flat made its familiar clunking noise. I lived in a prefabricated concrete block on an estate with dozens of such blocks scattered around a wasteland. They were noisy, ugly, crowded places, the sort of eyesores which deserve only the bulldozer. But friends and colleagues were envious of what to me was my tiny flat; all that space to myself, and a telephone as well. What privileges. Indeed, it was much more than most other people had.

I looked through the spyhole of the front door but as usual couldn't make anything out. I dressed and opened the door. Four men and a woman, all strangers. The woman – short, stumpy, wearing a pair of mid-calf boots then the height of fashion, had sharp bright eyes – simply said, 'I am Captain Barbara Pawłowska of the Polish State Security Service. May we come in?'

I can't remember now what my feelings were at that moment. The police visit wasn't entirely unexpected. Since August 1980 I had been writing freelance articles for *The New*

Statesman, The Observer and a variety of other journals, feeding them a regular supply of pieces about the free trade union organisation Solidarity, martial law, and other issues in Poland. I had done research for a BBC drama-documentary on the imposition of martial law, and generally developed a range of contacts and experiences not necessary for the teaching of Pinter and Beckett to third-year students of English. Moreover, I had just returned from England after a short break at Easter, and on first turning the key in the lock of my Bydgoszcz flat I felt something was up. The key had turned unusually smoothly in the lock, and traces of oil were around it. I thought someone had entered my flat but could see nothing untoward inside.

Now that it was actually happening it was still a shock. I began to tremble violently, the shaking made worse by my trying to get a grip on myself and hide my feelings from my unwelcome visitors. Police the world over are the same types. They understand the shock value they can have on people, they use their presence, their physicality, to intimidate and distress.

Pawłowska and her team entered. My flat was in its usual mess, books and clothes scattered everywhere. She introduced an interpreter – whose name I cannot recall, but I remember him saying he had come down from Warsaw – which was fortunate because my in any case indifferent Polish vanished completely under the stress of the incident. Pawłowska marched into the kitchen as though she owned the flat – as indeed she did, being a Polish taxpayer who was indirectly contributing to my rent-free status – and, when she saw the week's dishes stacked up, summoned up all her available sarcasm to say: 'You don't seem to get many young ladies round here, do you?'

I was allowed to make one telephone call to bring a fellow lecturer round to sit in on the search of my flat. I called on an American then teaching with me at the Wysza Szkoła Pedagogiczna – a kind of teacher-training establishment where I was then the British Council's Senior Lecturer in English Literature. There was no maltreatment, just Pawłowska's sarcasm and verbal intimidation. Her boys were cock-a-hoop, imagining, I guess, that they had captured an important spy, rather than a menial lecturer who had a journalistic sideline.

Gary Mead

By May 1983, when I was arrested and first charged, I had begun to understand some of the complexities not just of Communist Poland but of Eastern Europe generally. In theory I was there to help educate young Poles in English studies; given the handicaps they and I faced in that business, goodness knows if anyone really benefitted. Rather than they being educated it felt as though it was in fact a completion of *my* education, in history, politics, economics – in people.

The British Council had tried to convey the degree of culture shock which new lecturers were likely to experience in Poland, but in September 1979 I was completely unprepared for the sheer isolation I felt in my first few months in Bydgoszcz. The previous Bydgoszcz WSP lecturer had landed the post in Lublin, and thus managed to escape what turned out to be a very unpleasant working environment in the English department I was attached to.

My title – senior lecturer – was, I think, bestowed more to impress the Poles than anything else. The benefits for a Polish English department of having a British Council lecturer were many: access to books; the presence of a 'native speaker' of the language; financial and administrative support; but most of all an intangible kudos deriving from that tenuous connection with a recognised institution supported by British taxpayers.

The reality was that I parachuted into a department then run by two Polish academics, a husband and wife team, whom I fairly quickly and privately dubbed Mr and Mrs Macbeth. There were other junior lecturers but all, to varying degrees, were conscious that their jobs and future prospects were dependent on keeping their noses clean and not upsetting the Macbeths. It seemed to me all their energies were devoted to feathering their own nest, by getting themselves scholarships in the US or Britain, by organising timetables to minimise their own teaching loads, and by recruiting incompetent but nonetheless loyal junior staff. Given that I was unable to disguise these judgements, we did not enjoy the best relations.

Mrs M was in charge of the literature section of the Department, her husband the linguistics side. She and I clashed almost immediately and continued a desultory sniping war throughout my time there. One of my more enjoyable tasks was the teaching of drama, from Shakespeare to Pinter. Mrs M drew up her lecture list at the start of each year, as we were all required to do. Hers slavishly followed the dictates laid down by the syllabus requirements emanating from the Ministry of Higher Education in Warsaw.

I followed my own sophisticated educational theory, based on seeing what textbooks were available in multiple copies in the library – the only access students had to textbooks – and drawing up a list according to what students could *actually* get hold of. This, I quickly learned, was heresy. For one thing, it meant that I was omitting from my classes all references to that essential text, *School for Scandal*. Without a knowledge of Sheridan, the students would fail to comply with ministerial regulations, we would be graduating students who had not completed all the requirements; where would it all end?

I told Mrs M that I would not teach anything the students had no means of reading for themselves. She insisted that I at least tell them the plot of the play. I couldn't stop smiling. Coming from a Leavis-infused background and being naturally inclined to self-confidence, I though this sounded like insanity and refused.

My mutiny resulted in a protracted guerilla war between me and the Macbeths, culminating (I was told by the Warsaw HQ) in Mrs M suggesting to the British Council that it might like to replace me with someone more competent. Fortunately the Council was then – when isn't it? – facing a cost-cutting round dictated by the first Thatcher government. Mrs M was told that if Mead went, no one would replace him. She saw which side her bread was buttered on; open warfare ceased, replaced by a terrorist campaign waged behind the scenes. Mrs M was completely obsessed with the post-modern American novel; I swear she had a scrapbook with photos of Thomas Pynchon, John Barth et al. glued in it. I amused myself by telling students that America had only one novel of any significance, *Huckleberry Finn*. If pushed, I would admit Ed McBain into the canon.

My life in the Department became much easier with the return from a US sabbatical of the true head of the English faculty, Aleksander Szwedek, a man of considerable personal ability and integrity, who after the end of martial law took

Gary Mead

charge of the more recently-opened English Department at Toruń University, some 40 kilometres from Bydgoszcz. In my day, it had been a high-level political decision to site the English Department at Bydgoszcz, rather than Toruń. Bydgoszcz was being rewarded for its political conformity, Toruń punished for its history of student activism. In 1979, no one in their right mind would have chosen to live and work in Bydgoszcz, whereas Toruń even then was a pretty, interesting and more lively place to be.

Szwedek and I became good friends as well as colleagues. He completely supported me in my teaching and, later, in my journalism, though I never confided in him anything more than the broad outlines of my activities. He was in 1979 what might be termed a critical member of the Communist Party, a member but in open disagreement with its corruption. He took an active role in Solidarity when it started in August 1980 and left the Communist Party in December 1981 when it imposed martial law, a courageous act of defiance which might have meant dismissal from his job. I was immensely grateful to him for his behaviour following my arrest in 1983. He continued to invite me to his home and was happy to be seen in public with me.

My first year was a struggle, not just with the Macbeths but with all aspects of life, material and social. Unable to sleep, I would often be awake in the early hours of the morning, making cups of tea and reading. From my kitchen window, high above the tiny cluster of crude shops near my block, I would see women huddled in front of a butcher's, even though the temperature had fallen to minus 10 degrees centigrade and the snow was thickly falling. They were the professional queuers, waiting for the shop to open hours later.

Supermarkets rarely had more on their shelves than turnip oil, vinegar, poor quality cheese, eggs and bread. There were shortages of everything, not just meat – which I bought only twice in my first year – but also toilet paper, matches, even potatoes. Vodka was the one item that was always available. Once a consignment of Greek tinned peaches hit my local supermarket; a memorable occasion, not least because the colourful wrapper was itself a delightful change from the normal drab reality.

Vodka played an enormous symbolic role in Poland when

I was there. People outside Poland now forget that Solidarity was much more than a trade union. It also delved into the social and cultural devastation wrought by corrupted socialism. It carried out research into alcoholism, discovering that in 1981 10% of Polish society was regularly drunk every day. It would have been easy to turn alcoholic. I contented myself with a bottle of Russian champagne most evenings in my first few months, then gradually found I hardly drank at all. Instead, I smoked heavily, though I could never adjust myself to local brands such as 'Sport' or 'Caro'.

But the turning point for me, the event which gave my life meaning in Poland, was – and I apologise to my former employer for saying so – the start of Solidarity. I was never more than marginally involved in the organisation itself, though as a teacher I was invited and did join my local branch and paid my subscriptions[1]. But I became fascinated by it, observing its strengths and absurd failings. One of the many sayings which gained currency at the time was that Solidarity was a 'giant with clay legs' and after a while I always had the image of a Golem when I thought of the union, a created being which had little control over itself and its actions.

When Solidarity hit the world headlines I was in a dilemma. I wanted to write about it, but how? All the major media had their correspondents on the ground and besides that the Council contract forbade involvement in the 'political life of the host country', a broad stipulation which was my final undoing. At the same time I found myself irritated at the British press, which portrayed Solidarity as another brave-but-doomed insurrectionist Polish movement, exploding from nowhere and headed towards the same place. My first year – 1979 – in Bydgoszcz, a much harsher environment than Warsaw or Kraków, the cosmopolitan haunts preferred by journalists, diplomats and, it must be said, Council staff, laid bare the reasons behind Solidarity's instant success. The whole fabric of society was in terminal collapse. People were on the verge of malnutrition, hospitals were a disgrace, the values commonly encountered were cynicism, exasperation and bitterness.[2]

So in August 1980 I decided to write a piece which would try to explain the background problems – what I might now call

Gary Mead

a 'news analysis' piece – and to send it to *The New Statesman*, as the place most likely to be poor enough to be interested in a cheap but able foreign correspondent. That anonymous piece appeared on August 20 1980; the magazine told me it wanted more.

Thereafter I used a pseudonym, 'Gustaw Moszcz', formed from my initials and the last syllables of Bydgoszcz. A Polish colleague found it somehow appropriate, saying that 'Moszcz' meant 'must', the stuff that drops to the bottom of vats in wine-making. I immediately thought it could mean 'scraping the barrel'; certainly *The New Statesman* must have thought that apposite, given the unprofessional lengths, styles and modes of my filings. But for me it was an apprenticeship in journalism.

When I was unceremoniously permitted to leave Poland almost four years later I learned that my apprenticeship had been served with – literally – poor masters. By that stage I was also regularly writing for *The Observer*, under the byline 'Feliks Polonski' – another joke, this name meaning the 'happy Pole'. On my return to England in August 1983 I saw both *The Observer* and *The New Statesman*. Unemployed and without even a type-writer (confiscated by Captain Pawłowska as 'evidence'), I was desperate for a job. Neither offered me one, both pleading the poverty of their resources. It was a bitter homecoming.

By 1981 my circle of friends and contacts had expanded and life become much richer, socially if not materially. The upheavals in Poland, the constant knife-edge tussles between the Communist state apparatus and Solidarity, gave everyone who lived through those days considerable anxiety but also, I think, a heightened sense of meaning and purpose, as if the country had awoken from a lengthy stupefaction. Teaching was more enjoyable as I grew in confidence; my doctorate lay unregarded in a metal trunk, while I spent my spare time scooting round the country with Polish friends, interviewing, making contacts and learning what was going on and why.

I was never optimistic about Solidarity's long-term future, but the end came in bizarre fashion. On Saturday December 12 1981 I borrowed a small Fiat to drive from Bydgoszcz to Warsaw, where I was due to meet and interview the dissident Adam

Michnik. He had promised to spill the beans concerning a disturbing development within Solidarity, a growing anti-Semitism in some of the union's regions. But at Michnik's flat he cried off, saying he just had to go to the US Embassy to see a film about the Russians in Afghanistan. 'Come back next week, there will be plenty of time then,' he said.

Disappointed, I set off back for Bydgoszcz. By that time, late at night, the snow was falling thick and fast. Driving conditions were appalling but the five hour journey was broken up by military convoys, all heading into Warsaw. Long lines of trucks, interspersed with the occasional armoured vehicle, every fifty miles or so. It seemed very suspicious but I got back to Bydgoszcz safely, without being stopped, in the early hours of Sunday.

So I slept through the first moments of martial law. On Sunday December 13 I woke at about 10am, fried some bacon and eggs, switched on the radio to listen to the BBC World Service, certainly the greatest single comfort during my time in Poland. I had already tried to make a phone call, but the line was dead. That was unusual but, given the decrepit nature of the Polish telephone system, more a nuisance than a cause for alarm. Then I heard the BBC news, the newsreader delivering the thrilling, frightening and, to me, not unexpected bulletin: military rule in Poland, thousands believed arrested, some deaths reported in the south of the country at a coal mine, the banning of Solidarity, the sealing off of the country from the rest of the world.

It was a terrible time. My closest friend in Poland, Grzegorz Drymer, a colleague in the English Department, who now works for the BBC in London, was arrested in the early hours of the morning, wrenched from his wife and very young baby. It felt terrible, being unable to help them, or any other Polish friends.

I knew that I would stay as long as I was able and somehow try to write what I could, and get it out of the country. By this stage of my journalism I knew the wife of a Council employee in Warsaw; she offered to send mail for me through the British Embassy's diplomatic bag. We never discussed what the mail was. That was useful, though it was a nuisance having to travel to Warsaw once a week and then to make surreptitious contact with my Council helper.

Martial law meant curfews, grimly black jokes, furtive meetings, wild rumours and much misery for many ordinary people who had simply tried to lead a decent life. I went to Warsaw just before Christmas and at the Council I was told by a Council official to go along to the British Embassy as the defence attaché wanted to see all us lecturers, individually. People like contract lecturers from provincial backwaters like Bydgoszcz were, under normal circumstances, beyond the ken of military attachés, but these were strange times. At that moment conditions were so grim that we had been granted the very useful privilege of being able to buy things from the Embassy shop, a real treat to be taken advantage of whenever in Warsaw. So we had a legitimate reason to be scurrying to and from the Embassy.

Dressed in my winter clothes – skinhead-type boots, ex-RAF greatcoat, black woolly hat – I presented myself at the Embassy one morning, when the snow was still lying thick and soft. I was quickly ushered into the presence of the military attaché, Group Captain Wally Mears: at least that was how he was introduced to me.

The Group Captain was clearly having a whale of a time. A luxurious camp bed was made up in front of a roaring fire, in an enormous room, on a grand scale which for a moment was difficult to take in; I had become accustomed to tiny rooms with ceilings crowding down. Coffee was ordered and the Group Captain proceeded to his main theme, martial law.

A combination of lecture and grilling, his speech was animated. He told me that martial law presented the world with an excellent chance to gauge the reliability or otherwise of the Polish Army, to see just how many units would be mobilised, in what strengths, with what speed, and overall to construct a picture of the Polish military organisation.

He asked me what had been happening in Bydgoszcz. I gladly told him what I had observed, which was not much. The population had quickly thrown in the towel and there was little or no local resistance. As the interview wound up, Mears came out with his real purpose. Would I return to Bydgoszcz and make note of the insignia on military vehicles and of the ranks of those on street patrols and other such stuff? I left his office both excited and alarmed, and never saw him again.

I recalled the meeting with Mears in May 1983, when the Council told me it wanted to end my contract for breaking the clause which prohibited any political involvement in my 'host country'. My political involvement was wrong because I was caught; the kind Mears requested was not wrong because it was never discovered.

In the heady first weeks of martial law British Council lecturers were in an advantageous position, able to travel freely round the country so long as we had the necessary permit, whereas foreigners based in Warsaw, including accredited journalists, were restricted to the capital. On one visit to the Council's HQ on Jerozolimskie Street in late December 1981, I was surprised to be taken by a Council officer to a room where correspondents from the BBC, ITN and *The Times* were sitting, ready and waiting for lecturers like myself to drop in and give them a briefing on what was happening in parts of the country they could not see for themselves. As far as I was concerned this was not only breaching our contract and thus threatening our employment; it was also taking a good story away from me. I made my excuses and left after a few minutes.

Journalists based in Warsaw showed no hesitation in exploiting what some of us lecturers had seen or heard; one of my colleagues, based in Gdańsk, had taken some marvellous photos of peaceful protests in Gdańsk, which ended up on the front pages of the world's press – for which he received neither credit nor cash. So it was my experience that, unpalatable as this may still be to the British Council, its officials in Warsaw were willing to act as conduits between the British intelligence services and the media and ordinary contract lecturers. I was, however, already playing that game, on my own terms and for my own purposes.

In the early days of martial law I spent much of my time gathering the most accurate information I could obtain. Networks of rumour and gossip, some of it well-founded, sprang up very rapidly although it was evident that Solidarity's leadership, which by December 1981 had grown rather complacent, had no forewarning of the coup which, for the time being, cut its legs away on December 13.

About 10,000 people were arrested across Poland, many, like my friend Grzegorz Drymer, held in makeshift camps far from their families. My Christmas that year was, paradoxically, rather wonderful. I spent it with a married couple who were close friends of mine at the time. She was a judge and very highly-strung, anxious that her husband, a philosophy lecturer, was about to be arrested. But the secret police rather accurately assessed the danger he represented – zero – and left him alone. We spent the night before Christmas eating fish and mushrooms, drinking scotch and talking, eventually taking lots of fish and cream to feed the hordes of stray cats who inhabited the cellars of their building. Outside, armoured cars patrolled the streets, shining their searchlights into the faces of passers-by, the curfew temporarily lifted for Christmas.

By late December I decided to return to Britain for a brief spell, to have a break and also to write up the material I had gathered. Despite it being three weeks since the coup, the British media were still fascinated by the Polish situation, the fascination lingering (I suspect) because the military authorities had done a very effective job of clamping down on all information. No telephones, no post, no travel, nothing.

I travelled home via the port of Szczecin, taking a ferry to West Germany. I went through Polish customs loaded with notes, badges and other paraphernalia, and had hidden in my underpants a couple of copies of one of the first underground Solidarity publications, *Tygodnik Mazowsze*, which eventually became the best source of uncensored information in Warsaw. The trouble with all such publications is that one can rarely test the accuracy of the information they contain.

I passed the material on to a contact at the Polish section of the BBC, who in turn handed it to ITN's flagship news programme, *News at Ten*. That night I was amused to see Alistair Burnett wave aloft a few scraps of paper which earlier that day had been nestling in my underpants. His glee at the 'exclusive' might have been much less had he known the papers' previous home.

Martial law naturally gave extra scope for my journalism, though problems of delivery made it much more tricky than before. Having access to the diplomatic bag was invaluable, but it meant I was always writing analytical, rather than immediate news, pieces. As I wrote more, I also became more critical of Solidarity and its handling of events between August 1980 and December 1981. There was an unpleasant underside to the union which was rarely touched on then and has since, it seems, disappeared into the mists of history. Not only did Solidarity make some ridiculous decisions and act with remarkable naïveté, but it failed to organise when it had the breathing space to do so.

One example. Its national organising committee developed the farcical notion that if one of its members – and there were considerably more than 100 – dissented from a particular proposal, then that proposal would be defeated. Democracy was synonymous with complete unanimity, a crazy idea which inevitably led to paralysis. But we should not have been surprised by such a development. After all, in the 18th century Poland's nobility had created a similar principle, the *liberum veto*, enabling a single dissenting voice to cripple all legislation. That so weakened Poland's fragile democracy that it became ripe for dismemberment by its autocratic neighbours in the Partitions of 1772-95, which wiped Poland off the map for 123 years.

Jaruzelski's Communist-military government had no such organisational problems. This is not the place for an analysis of Solidarity, but my experience at the time led me to believe that its own internal incoherence assisted its defeat at the hands of a well-planned and well-implemented military coup. There were pockets of resistance to martial law, some of them relatively large, well-organised and determined. But what shocked me in Bydgoszcz was how easy it had been for the authorities to impose their will. My deduction, which might be unpalatable to those interested in recalling history through rose-tinted spectacles, was that Solidarity had spent too much time examining its own navel, and not enough putting down substantial roots.

All that is perhaps irrelevant. With hindsight one can dispute the assertion that Solidarity was, in many respects, an organisation which disappointed. Perhaps we should simply have rejoiced at its very existence, which so often seemed miraculous. I regard that as sentimental; it is too easy to give joy for miracles, too easy to gaze on them in wonder and fail to incorporate them into everyday existence. One of my biggest regrets is that I never got to ask Michnik to fully explain to me why some elements of Solidarity appeared to be entertaining anti-Semitic attitudes – a dark corner which probably cannot now ever be illuminated.

After Pawłowska and her boys finished searching my flat they took me into custody, stopping en route to let me buy some cigarettes. I had no idea how long I might be held.

At the Milicja HQ we drove in through large metal gates. In the cells, a uniformed guard took my name and address, asked me to hand him my shoelaces and belt – 'We cannot let you hang yourself' – and took me to my cell. I asked to be put in a cell by myself but he laughed and said something about not wanting me to be lonely.

I was allowed to keep toothpaste and toothbrush, cigarettes and matches, and a copy of Vera Brittain's *Testament of Youth*, and was put into a cell with two convicts. They turned out to be as nervous of me as I was of them, but after a few hours they began to initiate me into the ways of jail, such as how to conserve matches by splitting them. They also showed me how to make a fiercesomely strong brew of tea. They ripped a two-inch wide strip from my cotton sheet, spread it with duck-fat and rolled it tightly into a bandage-like roll. This they balanced on an inverted chair, beneath a zinc soup dish full of water and about half-a-pound of cheap tea. The home-made candle was then lit, the tea boiled and turned into a simple narcotic. They offered me first refusal.

I was kept inside for just three days – otherwise my cotton sheet would have completely disappeared. The food and accommodation were standard prison fare; horrible but not unbearable. On my last day the warder said what a pity it was I was leaving before lunch, and wouldn't I like to stay and join the others?

I was regularly taken from the cell and asked to confess to unspecified 'crimes' but I initially refused, instead asking what they thought I should confess to. I was denied contact with the British Embassy but assumed (correctly) that my American colleague had contacted the Embassy on my behalf.

In one session Captain Pawłowska became rather exasperated and stomped off, returning with a huge pile of typewritten papers. 'This is why you are here,' she said. I leafed through the papers and, for some inexplicable reason, smiled broadly. The pile comprised photocopies of what looked like every article I had ever written for *The New Statesman*, attached to each being a Polish translation of the article itself.

At that point I decided the game was up. I decided I might as well admit to writing those pieces and perhaps get out of jail sooner rather than later. I was formally charged and then released the next day into the hands of some splendid people from the British Embassy, who had driven up from Warsaw. They came armed with a large bottle of brandy, bananas, and some excellent sandwiches. We drove back to my flat and had a wonderful feast.

I cannot recall our conversation, except that it was rather innocuous and they seemed to enjoy their outing as much as I did mine. I then slept soundly for several hours, and later went out to buy a pickaxe handle from the local ironmongery. I kept it by my bed; too many people targetted by the régime had found themselves beaten up by unknown 'hooligans'. I decided to defend myself if the same happened to me. It never did.

Some days later the Council representative came to visit me. No bananas and brandy this time but instead a rather stiff conversation in which he tried to elicit from me what my plans were. Essentially it was a bartering session in which it was agreed between us that if I did not make a tabloid fuss, he would ensure that I was allowed to end my contract naturally – with three months' salary still to come.

My final weeks in Bydgoszcz, during May and June 1983, had an unreal air to them. The weather was glorious, sunshine every day, and I still had teaching commitments. My students looked on me with even greater curiosity than before, though they kept their distance, very sensible given my obviously contaminatory condition. I had become rather dangerous for many people to associate with; the couple with whom I spent Christmas 1981 walked past me on the street, an attitude I understood though thought foolish, since the police knew full well of our previous friendship.

Gary Mead

It didn't help that the police had confiscated from my flat my diary of two years under martial law – which I have never had returned to me. It was a fairly enigmatically written document but gave the police scope enough to haul in other people for questioning. It was no comfort to me on my return to England to know that no one lost their job or suffered in any way for my activities; the fear was always present for my friends and colleagues that something might happen to them as a result of their association with me.

Meanwhile, the alleged spy gave a run-down of imagery in the metaphysical poets and discussed the significance of memory in Samuel Beckett. The police couldn't believe their bad luck with me; here was a potential major spy, a career-maker, yet the evidence was paltry. I was required to go through a weekly farce of being interrogated by the public prosecutor in charge of my case, a highly unpleasant individual named Mr Obuchowicz.

I learnt from a friend that Obuchowicz was given to boasting how, in 1946, he had once dealt with a group of anti-Communist prisoners locked in a Bydgoszcz cell. I would visit this man, accompanied by my Polish lawyer. Obuchowicz always denied the lawyer access to the interrogation sessions, and I would then respond 'no comment' to each question.

This nonsense happened on three or four occasions until one day Obuchowicz announced: 'You are digging your own grave, Mr Mead.' To which I said: 'No comment.' On our final meeting he said that I was to be charged with another crime: 'Inciting Officers of the Polish Army to Mutiny'. This was a more serious charge since it carried a sentence of three-to-eight years, and anything above three years could not be suspended. If there were a trial I would (naturally) be found guilty and now would inevitably serve a minimum three years.

That was an unpleasant prospect but, although it might be difficult to believe, I really wanted a trial. I saw it as a vindication, a culmination almost, of my own drama. I was to be cheated of my wish, no doubt a lucky escape for both me and many others.

It all came to a fairly dismal end. A few days after my final encounter with Obuchowicz my lawyer said he had struck a deal, under which my passport would be returned and thus I would be able simply to drive across the border. I would not be stopped, although I was not officially being granted permission to leave the country. My lawyer told me to go. If I stayed and went for a trial it could get nasty for me and my friends. On a bright sunny day in early July I loaded up my car and drove via Poznań to East Germany, having said goodbye to my friends.

In my time in Poland all the relationships I formed seemed intensely powerful, though most have now petered out. I still don't know if what I did was right. Some months later I received a letter from the Bydgoszcz court telling me that I had been amnestied, but in the opinion of the court I was guilty as charged. It took me many months to stop missing Poland, the people I knew there; it took even longer to recover the same sense of meaning that I felt my life possessed when I was there. I went there as a teacher; instead I was the taught.

---

[1]   For a contemporary account of Solidarity's development in Bydgoszcz, see *The Polish House* by Radek Sikorski, Harper Collins, 1997. (ed.)

[2]   That is perhaps too harsh. Two other values were much in evidence throughout my four years in Poland. I met with astonishing courage and unstinting hospitality at all turns.

Sean Molloy

Specimen Days in Kraków

28 October 1983: My first full day in Poland. Perhaps my view is strongly coloured by what I've read and heard; undoubtedly the sombre late autumn weather shrouds most of northern Europe; but Warsaw does seem singularly doleful, in fact grey with trauma. Stalinist Palace of Culture and 'Free World' Forum Hotel brazenly dominate the skyline of central Warsaw, as if playing 'who-will-blink-first' across the prostrate cityscape. A scurrying nervousness in the air, a harassed furtiveness; martial law is still in force, after nearly two years. On the plane yesterday I read a piece by Waldemar Januszczak, who is of course of Polish parentage, telling of Poland's autumn ritual of mass wild mushroom picking. Apparently every year a handful of people die after eating the wrong fungi. Then this morning, at the British Council offices, one of the Polish secretaries told me that her young daughter is in hospital with fungus poisoning. In a strange country one is impelled to look for clues to the 'national character', keys to the collective myths, turning to allegory every story, every anecdote, every joke, every passing incident; it's an attempt to anchor oneself. So my imagination sets to work on this story of the poisoned girl (who soon recovers): a reckless people, addicted to risk? a people driven by a powerful pastoral nostalgia, by a legend of the good (blood-fertilized?) Polish earth and what it brings forth? a relatively unconsumerized, unsupermarketized people, hunters, foragers, gatherers rather than shoppers? But this is mostly guesswork; wild mushrooms are very good to eat. *Never* 'change money' in the street, in an hotel, etc., someone warns me.

Shopping, which I dislike even in the opulently-stocked

Sainsbury's, Safeway's, etc., is already becoming a motif. I am taken by my British Council 'shepherd', Anne Coneybeare, to the British Embassy Shop, to which lecturers have recently been granted limited access. Anne strongly advises me to stock up on such goodies as citrus fruits and bananas, chocolate, good wine ('And vodka?' 'No,' says Anne, no shortage of good vodka anywhere in Poland), toilet rolls.

Evening express to Kraków, crammed with travellers. Six of us shoulder to shoulder in a first-class compartment, and smokers elbow to elbow the length of the train's corridor. Evidently Poles are more relaxed about physical contact with strangers than are the British. Opposite to me a sturdy woman helps her pretty teenage daughter with exercise book maths. I am very dry so take from my bag an Embassy Shop orange. Is it my imagination, or are mother and daughter stealing longing glances at the fruit as I devour it? Wonder if I should proffer one of my precious oranges. In Africa or Arabia I should certainly do so but here I am unsure of the etiquette, don't want to offend. Shamefacedly creep into the corridor to finish my orange among the smokers. 'Change money?' whispers someone.

Ewa – a colleague-to-be – who meets me at the station, says she was easily able to pick me out from the struggling, laden crowds by a certain indefinable 'westernness' which hangs about me. I note the notorious Kraków air; it has body, personality, presence, never could you refer to it as 'thin air'. Ewa tells me that this time of year is the worst atmospherically, 'the most dangerous'. England's pea-soupers of the early 1950s, which I am old enough to remember, were also at their most lethal in late autumn/early winter; also evocative of Attlee's and Churchill's Britain are the troops of smokers and the military policemen prowling in threes, sniffing out AWOL national servicemen.

Ewa and her husband Grzegorz take me by Polski Fiat to the name-day party of Grzegorz's sister. The party has been going on for several hours and many of the celebrants are well on in drink, though no one is drunk. An animated but even-tempered political argument breaks out between Grzegorz, who is Solidarność, and his sister, who is Party. As the party breaks up I perform *Bruderschaft* – a linking of arms, a drink, a swift bout of necking – with two or three of the women. A promising start,

Sean Molloy

on the whole, to life in Kraków. I wonder if this first day will turn out to have been an overture, heavy with themes which will be developed, recapitulated, varied as days and weeks go by.

8 November 1983: To Collegium Novum, on the fringe of the Stary Miasto (the Old City), for my first lecture, on Thomas Hardy. I wish this splendid (19th century mock-Gothic) edifice, most of whose elegant rooms seem to be given over to Administracja, housed the Instytut Anglistyki, which endures a kind of internal academic exile in the drab Institute of Foreign Languages just off the main Warsaw road; the tail is wagging the dog. Plumb in the centre of my blackboard, a single graffito, Solidarność, which I completely ignore; I have been told/warned that every group of, say, thirty-five students will most likely harbour a police inform- ant. About forty students, docile, attentive, several exceptionally fine young women. I focus on *Tess of the D'Urbervilles*, a set book. When I ask for questions the students want to know if I can get hold of a video of Polanski's *Tess*, for showing at the Institute.

15 March, 1984: The cursed shopping so vexatious that I hardly ever cook for myself; no fresh fish to be had, epic queues for meat, which is still rationed, all this of course *déjà vu* from austerity Britain. I am tending to eat out five or six evenings a week, sometimes twice in a day, lunch and supper, usually at one of the state-run hotel restaurants, which are at least reliable and always have beer. They're beyond the financial reach of most Poles and certainly of most of my Polish colleagues, so this of course is becoming a source of guilt (the orange-on-the-train syndrome), as is buying German beer, Spanish wine, occasional- ly chocolate at the Pewex (hard currency shop). In the pitiable Polish shops (in the Jubilat 'superstore' you often have to queue for twenty minutes for your wire basket) us 'westerners' are tempted to assume a Harrod's/Fortnum's-customer hauteur in the face of the poverty of what is on offer and the sulky assist- ants, although our own natural shopping habitat is probably the Co-op. The Poles suffer from a scarcity-neurosis, running and struggling frantically to be first on to empty buses and trains, almost sexually wedged together by anxiety as they queue. A visual motif of my time here will be that of *The Struggling*

Crowd, lurching from one petty frustration to the next, a postscript manqué – 'The Disempowered Crowd' – to Elias Canetti's *Crowds and Power*, which studied French revolutionary crowds, Nuremberg, etc., powerful crowds. I am invited to 'change money' right outside the State Bank.

My Polish colleagues are mostly working mothers in their thirties and forties. Some have American accents, some RP, some faintly Slav, but all of those to whom I have spoken speak excellent English. Many of my colleagues, of either sex or whatever age, seem harassed, crestfallen, trammelled by circumstance. Two or three of the male junior lecturers are full-blown young fogeys, and around the Department generally 'socialism' is a dirty word, the assumption being, as among Thatcherite Conservatives and Reaganite Republicans, that there is little or nothing to choose between social democrats and Communists. I suppose I was half-prepared for such attitudes, but I wasn't ready for the pervasive political solipsism here, founded on a national Catholic myth of Martyred Poland and an intense hatred of the Soviet Union. From this it follows that liberal 'westerners' i.e., a majority of the teachers and lecturers who come to Poland – are for their Polish hosts exasperating naïfs. Poland yearns to come into her Western and European birthright, her recognition as the West's easternmost bulwark, for a millennium *Antemurale Christianitatis*; but for many Poles the West, in 'betraying' Poland, not only nor most recently at Yalta, has betrayed its own best self. In *Wśród Polaków* (*Among the Poles*, title of one of my Polish language primers) one discerns a certain proud, tacit contempt; shopping has softened up the West, turned us into gratuitous spectators at Poland's austere, passionate drama. The implicit corollary (Dostoyevskian, ironically) is that suffering has made the Poles a great-souled people. Poland's history, as well as her religion, drives the Poles to try to escape from history, into typology; they hold fast to the idea of man's essential nature, and woman's, which leads them to scoff at feminism. 'Change money?' – on Ulica Floriańska. I have become an experienced refusenik.

1 May 1984: Our political differences notwithstanding, many of my Polish fellow-lecturers are very matey. Their general culture turns out to be not élitist but popular, 'common' in the Raymond

Sean Molloy

Williams sense, including an unaffected love of football, or beer, an educated taste in American popular song – Gershwin, Porter, Rogers and Hart – or in jazz. Today, as I watch the 'spontaneous' marchers and flag-wavers, I am greeted in the street by the linguist Rafael Konopka, a bit of a Cold War warrior but highly affable. May Day, says Rafael, is in the nature of a sacrilegious holiday of obligation. He also tells me, as medical fact, that Kraków's air is likely to damage the health of anyone who spends most of his time here over a period of three to four years. The smokers, says Rafael (of whom he is one) are fatalistic; what harm in the odd calming ciggy when the city is doing them in anyway? Certainly there seems to be a lot of sickness here, much of it, I would guess, psychosomatic, a dystopia of 'flus and rheums and agues and fluxes, a sick-note pandemic. The late Renaissance, Italianate Old City fans out in four directions from the huge Rynek (main market square) which has at its heart the Sukiennice (Old Cloth Hall), which enshrines a lovely old gallery of mellow-lit shops, and in one corner the darkly radiant Mariacki – St Mary's Church – which has two spires, from the upper reaches of one of which, every hour on the hour, day and night, year in year out, a trumpeter plays a plaintive melody, abruptly broken off on about the eleventh bar, commemorating the trumpeter who, in this city in the 13th century, was killed in mid-warning of invasion by a Tartar arrow in the throat. The Old City is environed by a green belt (Planty) but the crumbling of the fine old houses, the University colleges, the score or more of churches and the Wawel Castle which commands the Vistula – the sinister crumbling proceeds visibly, palpably. On a clear day, they tell me, from certain vantage points around Kraków you can see the Tatra mountains. But if you take a tram to the Salwator church then climb up Aleja (George) Waszyngtona to the massive Kościuszko mound you can see the riverine trough in which Kraków lies, and the shiftless haze which is claiming the city. Here heavy weather hangs about; but the source of most of the air and water pollution is Nowa Huta, built during Poland's Stalinist era about a dozen tram-stops east of historic Kraków as a kind of workers' watchdog over the recusant city of old Catholic families, of professors and doctors and their ladies, of lingering Austro-Hungarianisms. As such, though with age the watchdog has taken several bites at the hand that feeds it, Huta is resented and despised by almost all *echt* Krakówians. But the steel town is also the source annually of six or seven million metric tons of steel. It all comes down to filters, as in cleaned-up Sheffield, which the steel works managers say they cannot afford or cannot afford to use. So the State fines the State-owned factory. This is the sort of detail which will keep a free-marketeer chuckling for months.

27 May 1984: My birthday (cards from my wife and sister and one from my old friend Mitch, addressed to 'Sean Molloy, Bringer of Shakespeare to the Melancholy Slav'; I recall that when I worked in Sudan Mitch sent a card to me as holder of 'The Mad Mahdi Chair of American Literature') and also my final seminar of the academic year, held at my flat. After the seminar, a few bottles of wine and beer, sandwiches and cakes. The students tell me that Poland will cure me of even my moderate socialism; once again the inverted vanity of the martyr. I tell them that it is possible to dislike both Thatcherism and Polish Communism, that Stalin's (and Hitler's) first victims were the social democrats, and that in Britain they themselves would line up on the left; they ponder this idea and say that yes, they probably would. I find them to be excellent company, especially after a few glasses. The party develops nicely into singing, then degenerates into joke-telling. The teaching has been very pleasant.

13 December 1984: Third anniversary of the imposition of martial law. The murder of Father Popiełuszko by agents of the State has begun to feel like a watershed, a real and crucial blow after years of State/Church shadow-boxing. It hands all the moral advantage to the Church, vindicating Cold War warriors of the West and winning sympathy for the Church among those who dislike its reactionary moral absolutism; and of course it simply blows away the arguments of those who have suspected that State and Church – rival totalitarianisms with certain areas of common interest (as Orwell always insisted) – were secretly complicit. An event like this is precisely what the régime didn't want, for its whole strategy has been based on keeping its power latent. And the symbolism – the killing of one of Jan Paweł's priests –

couldn't be more lurid, much worse for the régime than the slaying of, e.g., a student; as in Western Europe and the Americas there is in Poland a vague but potent popular feeling that students are spoilt, idle troublemakers.

17 March 1985: In terms of the calender of saints, the Poles are very learned. Patrick's Day falls during the conference to honour the seventieth birthday of Professor Przemysław Mroczkowski, for many years Pan Direktor of the Institute of English. The conference is an affair of great academic pomp and circumstance, calling out all that is venerable and Latinate and immemorial in the Jagiellonian University (founded 1371); the conference is also at times – I do not patronize – quaintly moving. Professor Mroczkowski is universally credited with having kept English studies in Kraków alive at a time when they were almost proscribed. His politics – founded, I think, on a nostalgic medievalism and the idea of Christendom – and his literary preferences – for Newman, Chesterton, the Anglo-Catholic inklings – are not my own, but I admire him for his defence of great literature and we share a liking for the poetry of Hopkins; my paper on GMH goes down well. On the evening of the Professor's actual birthday a buffet-reception is held for him outside Kraków at a most stately château, pre-Communism 'Big House' of some magnate. The party is very high-toned, with speeches in Latin, no less, and the general sense of an élite celebrating its own survival and its preservation of one of the kernels of independent intellectual life in Poland. The Catholic intelligentsia are a force here (still home to a vestigial religious fealty) and such things as this professorial party, the thriving churches whose congregations spill out on to the pavements, demonstrate the flimsiness of the Party's rule. The élan of Polish Catholicism is very striking; maybe its doctrinal affinities are with Franco's Spain, or even with de Valera's Ireland, but in Poland, not merely by virtue of its being in opposition, it escapes Francoesque dullness and conformism and appears to stand for gadfly wit and panache, for the quixotic subversion of all that is lumpen, dogmatic, un-Polish, for the spirit of Chopin against both Marxist and commercial materialism.

Professor Mroczkowski has been awarded the M(or O?)BE,

for services to English studies. Near the end of the seventieth birthday gathering the British Council representative makes a short speech adverting to this honour and then begins to open numerous bottles of champagne (or, strictly, *méthode champenoise*). A cork flies out precipitately and whizzes within inches of the head of Professor Mroczkowski, who is deeply absorbed in conversation and doesn't notice.

8 May 1985: A few hours in Warsaw, en route to Gdańsk to give lectures on Jean Rhys and on 'Eliot and Pound in London'. On the first of May I was in Zakopane where it snowed all day solemnly, implacably, and skiing was still in full swing. But the Polish spring, like the spring of Virginia and Maryland as evoked somewhere by Eliot, is explosive, and today Warsaw is sub-tropically hot. I am dying, therefore, for a beer, for several beers, but I don't want to go to a restaurant and on steamy, thronged Ulica Marszałkowska, in the only beer bar that this main drag can boast, I see one of the nervy but submissive crowd queues in which Poland specializes, drinker-penitents like NHS junkies at the midnight chemists, all men; four or five attendants, vigorous, elbowy women in their forties, bossy and officious as auxiliary militia. The drinker in me, never in perfect accord with the socialist, especially since I have outgrown simple pints-drinking, knows that Polish Communism has to go, even if succeeded by Catholic nationalism (driven along by the electronic Iron Maiden of Friedmanite economics). The Polish people are just so damned unhappy, their misery disturbing the after-dinner sleep of the West. The system makes them unhappy, and it makes them unwell; they want their slice of the cake ('What do we want?' said a young woman student to me. 'We want a bloody fucking slice of the cake!') even if it disagrees with their systems. The men and women of the Party have delivered cheap and plentiful public transport, free-at-the-point-of-use health care (though not always bribe-free), education to at least the age of eighteen for nearly everyone, nearly universal literacy, maternity and paternity leave; but in quenching Everyman's need for a few swift cold bevvies on a hot afternoon, Capitalism has outcatered them.

'Change money?'

Gdańsk, birthplace of Günter Grass (when it was Danzig),

is Hanseatic in feeling and architecturally akin to Copenhagen rather than to Kraków. I learn that this part of Poland used to be a separate province – Kashubia – and that Kashubians and the Kashubian language (a blend of Polish and German) still exist. From Gdańsk I go by night train to Lublin, then on to Kazimierz Dolny for a conference on 'Reception Theory'. Kazimierz is a handsome, rustic little town beside a broad stretch of the Vistula. Pre-War Kazimierz was about 80% Jewish; by 1945 it was entirely denuded of its Jews.

12 October 1985: Through my Fulbright colleague Ray Neinsteen, himself Brooklyn Jewish, I meet one of the very few young Kraków Jews, Henryk. Henryk, who works as a chemist, is a mild, modest, unremarkable man of about thirty-five who wears lightly his emblematic identity.

19 April 1986: With Ray Neinsteen and a few Polish colleagues I go by night train to Budapest for an American Studies conference. The border guards can be set in a paradigmatic triptych: Poles, regretfully dutiful; Czechs, gratuitously nasty; Hungarians, insouciant. In (relatively) prosperous Budapest it occurs to me that the Hungarians figure for the Poles much as the Spaniards used to for the French, the Danes for the Swedes, the Austrians for the Germans, Africa for Europe, black America for white: as libidinous other self.

10 June 1986: One of my M.A. supervisees has married a young American who has just completed his medical studies in Kraków and is about to return, with his bride, to the States, where in a year or two he may practice. Ray Neinsteen – the thesis reviewer – and myself are invited to the wedding/farewell party. This is a swish affair – real champagne, smoked salmon, olives (a very rare treat in People's Poland) – but Ray and I can't help but entertain dark suspicions about this marriage: it has the lineaments of a passport-and-citizenship job, in this case without the husband knowing. Such 'marriages', usually with money changing hands, are a well-established racket in London, especially around Earl's Court.

7 January 1987: Thirty-seven degrees below! Faces of people in the streets look flayed. Two pairs of sturdy trousers are not enough; the cold attacks knees, which begin to deliquesce. My beard freezes up, its appearance alarming passing children; I must look to them like the Bad Angel of the North, St Nicholas's fallen brother. Students in the Institute remain fully clothed all day, with chattering teeth, and air of rueful wretchedness but also a certain masochistic satisfaction. It is dangerous to be out and about; one could lose an ear or, like the granite bust of the writer 'Boy' Welensky in the Planty, one could lose the end of one's nose.

3 May 1987: I am in Karpacz, near the mountains of southwest Poland, for the annual British Council literature seminar. This year's rubric is 'Modern Critical Theory & Feminism'. Two lecturers have come from Warwick University (where I studied in the late '60s), one a radical feminist who refers scornfully to 'heterosex'. The weather is very fine, so many of our meetings are *sur l'herbe*, with a wistful view of distant hills. The erudite feminist lady sits under a tree surrounded by a little flotilla of young British feminists who are teaching English in Poland. Other sessions are led by Professor John Goode, a humanist Marxist, school of Raymond Williams. It irks me that none of the Polish lecturers, whom I know to be extremely hostile to even the mild, undogmatic Marxism of John Goode, challenges him; instead they chunter and rhubarb mutinously over breakfast or lunch: 'how can he believe such things? how can he say such things, in Poland?' At the end of the seminar an uninhibited party which culminates in small-hours singing and dancing in the pine forest which overlooks Karpacz village. An eerie atmosphere – thunder and lightning but no rain – redolent of 'What the Thunder Said'. John Goode is in the thick of the party but after he has departed for Warsaw I am astonished to learn that he is one of the longest-surviving heart-transplant people in the world.

25 May 1987: Auschwitz. I have put off coming here for more than three years. But Oświęcim is also an unselfconscious little town.

2 June 1987: After two years of supervision most of my Magister students have submitted their theses. I have always had high regard for this group and am very pleased by their work. The dissertations on Durrell, Golding, Woolf (two), Eliot's plays, Gerard Manley Hopkins and John Fowles are especially good. Best of all is a stunning piece of writing on Blake's *Prophetic Books*, by Leszek Smutek (Leslie Sorrow), who has become almost as fervent a Blakean as Kathleen Raine.

10 June 1987: Standing amidst dense crowds on the Błonia, the vast unenclosed grassland across from the Cracowia Hotel, I await the arrival of the Pope. While the Pope is in his homeland no Irish travellers (sic) are to be allowed in, and my neighbour, the timid Palestinian lecturer in Arabic, has been ordered by the police to remain in his flat throughout the Papal stay in Kraków. Hundreds of policemen, looking more than ever like off-duty criminals in mufti, line the streets; and the policewomen have all the drab glamour of cosh-boys' girlfriends in British crime movies of the '50s. The crowds are keyed-up to bursting. Hundreds of children are almost panting with excitement. As priests in surplices dart about, people of all ages drop to their knees and stick out their tongues, eyes closed, to receive the Host. The hand of a young fresh-faced priest finds the mouth of an old woman in a wheelchair, who then grasps in her large, strong, veined brown hands the priest's dainty white hand and brings it back to her mouth.

The sulky air is chopped into petulance as three helicopters approach from the East. They violently beat the air directly overhead. Many men shout, many women scream, children shriek, hundreds fall to their knees, crossing themselves. A woman with hair dyed auburn seems to pass out with rolling eyes, family catching her. I feel an atavistic awe, a tribesman on first seeing great thunder-birds in the sky. The helicopters touch down in a fenced-off area at the far end of the meadow and sit there like prizes in a fabulous lottery. A growling roar goes up as the Pope, in full pastoral robes and golden skullcap, emerges and kneels to kiss his native soil. The Pope is Poland's profile in the world and the world follows him to Poland; he is also, *mutatis mutandis*, the apotheosis of the European emigrant returned to the old country from a richer world. Down an avenue lined on both sides by lime trees in flower Jan Pawel is slowly driven in a long black limousine, smoked and bullet-proofed glass, four Vatican minders in black suits and glasses on the running boards, a dozen outriders on snarling motorbikes.

Papierz stands, glad-handing dignitaries of State and Church, on a raised platform in full view of the exultant crowds. There falls from the Holy Father a plenitude of benedictions. The mid-morning midsummer sun strikes directly at him as he stands calmly in vestments of white and cream and gold. I admire the Papal fortitude, though my unspoken impression is that Jan Pawel looks like a huge meringue. On the platform all sit except the Pope, who places himself confidently behind a microphone and speaks in a strong, carrying voice, his gestures few and emphatic, his oratorical style rhythmical and sonorous. The Pope speaks much of Poland's history and praises great Polish heroes of the past. He calls on everyone present, and on the greater Poland beyond this place and time, to remain true throughout all trials and crises to Poland's rich Catholic heritage, which is now as in times stretching back a thousand years the living heart of the nation. He says nothing of Communism nor of any modern political controversies, never alluding to abortion, or education, or martial law, or the murder by state policemen of one of his priests. But his audience, listening hard, taking everything he says allegorically, a schoolman's exegetists in the post-Kafka age, construe him in contemporary terms, laughing and exclaiming knowingly as they imagine the baffled fuming of the régime, one or two of whose representatives are sitting a few feet behind him. From its zenith the sun beats down on Jan Pawel's craggy Slav head, and still he speaks on, voice strengthening if anything, but gravely, soberly, no 'working' of the crowd. After some thirty minutes, his vigorous peroration met by crashing applause, he bestows a final blessing and turns his massive back. Later, footing it back to my flat – trams and buses are full, queues are endless – I perceive on many faces a certain rapt, lofty expression; destiny has touched them, drama has invested their obscure lives.

3 July 1987: Farewell party. Toasts and valedictory speeches, the singing of 'Sto Lat!'. I have enjoyed working here in Kraków and say as much in a brief effusion. Half a dozen of my colleagues have become good friends, with about a dozen more I am on very cordial terms; there are a number whom I barely know, and a handful to whom I have only spoken two or three times in more than three and a half years. One's feelings are always confused and cloudy at such times as this; gladness/sadness.

6 July 1987: Leaving Poland on a brilliant summer day, by car with my friend Angus Collins, British Council lecturer in Lublin. Our journey takes us through southern Poland, Czechoslovakia (Prague! ah, Prague! where we stay two nights), West Germany (remember?), Holland. To leave the last shabby Czech town and drive into the first gleaming West German village, to pass from eastern and central Europe into western Europe, is to go not so much from darkness to light as from neon-starvation to neon-satiation. Some Americans I knew in Kraków, on crossing this border, whooped and yelled and threw their remaining złoty – their poor old złoty! – to the winds; a sad triumphalism, Polish defeatism its unacknowledged brother. And yet, this is in part mere rhetoric; Poland in 1983-1985 had about it a feeling of defeat; by the middle of 1987 Poland was gathering her strength for another push and was eventually to fall through the door into an enormous unfurnished room.

Postscript: Specimen Days in Lublin

28 October 1988: I am back in Poland, in the old job and flat of Angus Collins, who is now in Japan. Late at night, fiddling with the dials on my radio, I hit a voice speaking English and listen to a report from Prague ladling derision upon 'student flunkers' and other 'blusterers' who have been demonstrating ('manifestating', as one of my students is later to describe parallel events in Wrocław) in Wenceslas Square. Things are looking up, patchily; today, without queuing, I bought half a kilo of lemons, but a few days ago I queued for half an hour to buy four toilet rolls, from a stationery shop. As I was poised to go through the door of the shop a rumour that the rolls were running out swept through the crowd and I was damn near trampled by a phalanx of robust grandmothers. Lublin is part of 'Poland Two', i.e. less prosperous than the towns of central-southwestern Poland, with an agricultural class which is observable at the open markets and around the bus station and which is still describable as 'peasantry'. But Lublin's air is fresh and it is a very wooded town; Złoty jesień (golden autumn) very beautiful here.

12 March 1989: One of the students wants to write about Orwell, for her M.A. I ask around the Department, 'Will that be okay?' and am given at first an amber, then a pale green light.

18 April 1989: With the writer and editor Jon Silkin and a couple of Polish colleagues, I go by cab to Majdanek. The camp is insolently close to the town and for me more chilling than Auschwitz; into some of the death-chambers the Germans built little observation-alcoves, room for two. Jon Silkin, who is Jewish, says little.

19 May 1989: On an early morning train journey from Lublin to Warsaw I have a compartment to myself, and no pesky muzak. I hear full-chested singing from the corridor and put out my head to see. A fat, grey-haired man, stuffed inside an abominable sweater, is standing Pavarotti-style, legs braced and arms beseeching, singing through an opened window his praises ('Uroda Polska!') to the Polish countryside. He glances round, sees me, coughs and quickly retreats to his own compartment. I note that he has a bad squint. I look out the window. The morning glows, poppies and other wild flowers. I see horse-drawn ploughs, kerchiefed old women bent double, old men and children standing to stare at the train, a young woman sitting under a massive tree to read, a dog rolling on its back. These are the most fought-across lands in Europe, bone in the soil, blood in the grain. Poland can touch you. I remember the Wajda-Cybulski film, *Ashes and Diamonds*, how it caught my imagination, showing a people brave, quirky, practical existentialists, throwing wit and style against tanks and realpolitik.

4 June 1989: Election Day; Free Election Day. It has been very moving to see the Polish people electioneering. Last week in

Sean Molloy

Warsaw I walked by the Party's campaign HQ; amplified pop music, pretty girls, razzmatazz. Evidently the Party thinks it is going to win! Cynically, the Party calculates that the electorate will 'hold on to nurse/for fear of encountering something worse'; but it won't.

3 March 1990: Near Lublin's Catholic University I see students from both it and the state university (my own Marie Curie-Skłodowska) laying non-violent siege to a large, stately building, Party premises. Nomenklatura hurry away with files and boxes. The students are satirical rather than belligerent.

20 October 1990: Signs and portents thicker than leaves will fall in Listopad (November). On Lublin's Ulica Lipowa farmers in bloodied white coats have set up little stalls to display and sell *al fresco* massive joints of beef and pork, cutting out the Man from the Ministry, his forms, his health checks. Everything in Poland has fallen off the back of a lorry; the country is in the throes of an orgy of petty trading, but the traders have no front, no chutzpah. At the centre of Warsaw station's booking hall sits a powerful, pampered car, to be won by lottery, and beside it a Romanian or gypsy beggar-woman, in thick coats and scarves, a child sleeping at her breast, rocks back and forth from the lotus position, lamenting and beseeching in the Latinate *lingua franca* of distressful Christendom. The trains are full of Russians, wedged in the corridors and up against the toalety, their cardboard boxes and shabby bags full of unsold goods, eating carp and sardines direct from the tin, with pocket knives. 'Da,' they say humbly as you struggle through. Soon the IMF bailiffs will stand where Hitler had dreamed of standing and the Sale of the Century – everything from cherry orchards to nuclear missiles – will commence. The Russians are here on Polish sufferance, the rouble much weaker than the złoty, the Russians' huge armies immobilized by capitalist enchantment. But the Poles do not gloat: they know what it feels like to be poor traders from the East. Kantor (money-changer) signs are everywhere yet still the 'change money' men stand outside the banks, looking like unhired longshoremen in *On the Waterfront*. The Unia Hotel in Lublin is hosting Poland's first-ever conference of Rotary

International: the little knots of Rotarians give off the soapy gleam of vindicated true believers, compulsive bestowers of the personalized business card. Graffiti; a yellow star of David inside a noose and, among wall after wall of presidential election posters, six-pointed stars upon the multiplied sea-turtle head of Tadeusz Mazowiecki; one of my colleagues at Marie Curie-Skłodowska tells me that 'Mazowiecki' is one of the ur-Polish names, while 'Wałęsa' is rooted in Polish denotations of 'the Wanderer'.

1 November 1990: All Souls' Day. In the still, twilit late afternoon the beautiful old graveyard on Lipowa is incandescent with a thousands-strong communion of many-coloured candles, flames barely wavering, their glow, their heat rising from the grave-stones and making radiant the middle air. The crowds who throng the bosky pathways are whole families, three or four generations strong, skippy children gently made grave by their elders. Many candles are in jars but most are as naked as the souls they symbolize. Some few flames will be kept from extinguishment month in month out, even on the grimmest winter days to come. Many headstones bear photographs, elaborate Christian insignia; some carry Battle of Britain aeroplane propellers. Here blazes a new memorial – to the Polish officers to whose slaughter at Katyn the Russians have as good as admitted. Here also is the Russian war memorial, a gigantic Red Army helmet cast in bronze, about a hundred graves, all dated July or August 1944; dark, candleless, wreathless. In another quarter of borrowed light there are mossy tumbled graves of the 18th and 19th centuries, inscriptions in Russian. Above them, on a little knoll, stands a ruined chapel. One small section of cemetery, well-lit and tended, plain headstones, ranks in the People's Army given, is Party; these graves are candle-bright and loaded with wreaths. I find myself walking towards General Jaruzelski, dark glasses, small entourage, still President for a few days or weeks. I think his mother rests in this soil.

4 April 1991: At the Unia Hotel I meet five or six Irishmen, in Poland to advise on the privatisation of banking (sic). A Polish-American banker who has been offering fabulous rates of interest has been arrested, his passport confiscated, and is arraigned on TV. Although he speaks fluent Polish he insists on (defiantly but unconvincingly) defending himself in English. Private English language schools are mushrooming; schoolteachers of the quondam compulsory Russian must convert to English. At the University's Institute of English there is excitement, but also apprehension; what will become of market-unfriendly specialisms like 'Transformational Grammar', or 'Medieval Eng Lit'?

30 April 1991: Two nights and a day in Kraków. The 'Holiday Hotel', once a lonely chunk of transplanted Americana, is asserting itself as a pattern of the new culture: roulette room; fashion shows; younger, smarter semi-resident prostitutes, fluent in English and German; slick waiters oozing sycophantic greed. Walking round old Kraków I feel at once exhilarated and saddened; what neglect had preserved, the booming tourism may splinter. Privation spread thin and wide had been for me part of Kraków's personality, although in Kraków I myself had been not much more than a glorified tourist, my claim on the city little stronger than that of the packaged cultural pilgrim, or even the international rubberneck. On this lovely spring day Kraków diffidently welcomes the pleasure-seeker, but Kraków can never be a playground. As native Poles weave hurriedly and worriedly through the crowds, I remember my first weeks in Kraków: crestfallen winter dawns, early afternoon twilights, bedrock snowbound nights. Today, in April, among my fellow amblers I see large groups of priests and nuns and I hear their Italian, which sounds dead right in this city; as does the Hebrew which I hear. About a third of the many scores of Jews wear orthodox dress. Probably the Vatican and Auschwitz will between them ensure that Kraków's charm remains sombrely decorous.

Stephen Romer

The Inner Station

By late July 1989, no one had yet applied for the post of Docent in English Literature at the Instytut Filologii Angielskiej in Łódź, Poland – a one year contract, renewable with the agreement of all parties. The idea of teaching in Poland had not crossed my mind until I rang the BC Literature Department in London and asked them to send me somewhere if they could, since the job I had been expecting in France had not materialized. This left me, late in the year, without a livelihood and a small family to support. Anyway, I called in at Spring Gardens, and if my memory isn't playing tricks, I seem to hear Harriet Harvey-Wood, in her inimitable way, looking up over her spectacles – 'So you're the poor devil going to Łódź?' Perhaps this is an embroidered retrospect... Half an hour later, I took away with me a fat dossier entitled *Poland*, prepared by the OEAD[1], which I read in a nearby pub. I ploughed dutifully through the conditions of service, climatic conditions, advice on clothing and vitamin supplements, and the vital necessity of equipping oneself with an all-purpose bath-plug. I read with some dismay the report of my predecessor concerning the state of the Docent's flat, but put that out of my mind, since the terms of service were decent, and there was a further inducement: in July 1989, Poland was hot news. The country was in the vanguard of democratic reform, and had a newly-elected, partially non-Communist government, under the premiership of that scholarly, and as it turned out, ill-fated man, Tadeusz Mazowiecki. Even so, few could have predicted the spectacular domino effect that was to ensue during the rest of that extraordinary year – with Hungary, Czechoslovakia, East Germany and Romania throwing off the

Communist yoke, while in Moscow, Mikhail Gorbachev, that ambiguous figure, stood by. He had spoken in Paris of our 'common European home', and as far as I was concerned Poland was one of the most exciting places to be in that fabulously enlarged Eldorado.

Time was pressing, so I signed a contract, without even looking Łódź up in a guidebook or on a map. When I finally did so, I found the place was given suspiciously short shrift, described as a one-time textile boomtown from the last century, but now, vastly expanded, in a state of decay. It is Poland's second city, with a population of some 850,000, situated 120 kilometers south-west of Warsaw. The most famous 'fact' about Łódź is its film school, a kind of secret enclave as I later found, where the likes of Wajda[2], Polanski and Kieślowski had cut their teeth. But as chance would have it, my first real glimpse of the city was in some dismal black and white photographs that accompanied an article in the travel section of *Le Monde*, entitled, unpromisingly, 'Łódź, la mal-aimée'. This made out that even the Poles were ashamed of their 'Manchester of the East'. The images showed ragged children playing in grimy 19th century courtyards, straight out of Dostoyevsky. There was also a shot of the interior of a textile factory; I thought of school-book illustrations of Bradford in the heyday of the Industrial Revolution.

The papers carried stories almost daily about staggering rates of inflation and food shortages in the New Poland, so as I waited for my visa application to go through I spent the time amassing supplies – a powerful radio, cereals, chocolate, coffee; lighters, biros, envelopes, paper; a czapka from Bates of Jermyn street. The day finally came, in late October, when I roped an iron trunk to the top of my Renault 5, and headed for the Harwich-Hamburg ferry. The journey out took on a decidedly Conradian aspect in my imagination – something like Marlow's trip to the inner station... Berlin Transit, the featureless landscape of the DDR, muffled with pine forest and an unspoken warning – 'Traveller Pass By'; there were signs to Leipzig and Dresden, but not for us. Queues of little multicoloured Trabis at the huge Intertank gas stations. Unsmiling frontier police. (When I returned that way in June 1990, on Reunification Day itself, the police had learned to smile, though the mask of newfound bonhomie kept slipping.) The Poles used to say of their East German neighbours – 'the bastards can even make Socialism work!' – but behind its screen of forest, the régime was tottering. Honecker stepped down in October 1989, shortly after that Judas-kiss from Gorbachev, leaving his dauphin Krenz in charge, former head of the Komsomol[3]; but that was not to last either.

In West Berlin I stayed with a friend, the Fluxus poet Emmett Williams, who had just been elected President of the (now flourishing) avant-garde Artists Gallery in Łódź; he chuckled knowingly when he heard where I was headed. In Berlin, the Poles were rapidly gaining a reputation as the most irrepressible black marketeers in Europe; miscellaneous markets spawned and dissolved in every open space in the city. Their speciality was transforming West German Mercedes' into Polish ones, complete with new plates and papers, in the space of minutes. I followed Zimmerstrasse, the little rat's alley that snaked along the Wall on its western side, one dark rainy night in late October. I examined the graffiti, the famous *Mauerkunst*, and startled rabbits in the no-man's land between Wall and tenement blocks. I drank beer in a dusty '60s-style pub near the Moritzplatz crossing-point. There was a large, threadbare pool table under a green-fringed lamp, and a Wurlitzer-type jukebox which was playing Humperdinck's[4] 'Please Release Me'. High above the crossing point were the silhouettes of armed guards in their watchtowers. It all seemed grotesque but unalterable; and yet barely a fortnight later pickaxes were at work, frenziedly smashing that Wall to pieces.

Out of Berlin, the signs read 'Polen VR'; and so to the long queues of Polish baby Fiats, freighted with merchandise, at the crossing point of Frankfurt an der Oder, and on to my first Polish road towards Poznań, narrow, lightless, with a broken macadam surface; heavy birch forest on either side. At Poznań, my first Grand Hotel, East European style, the first of many, gloomy, cavernous; the inevitable cloakroom, or szatnia, with its attendant crone; the cocktail bar full of tarts; a kotlet volaille which oozed rancid butter; and my first brush with the milicja, who demanded a fistful of dollars as a 'mandat' for 'illegal parking'. Then on to the awesome tower blocks of Warsaw, and a visit to the Council line-manager, who lived in a suburb behind barred

Stephen Romer

windows, purified his water twice, and seemed to live in terror of bugging devices. He gave me a potted history of Poland, facts and figures, advised against intimacy, and explained how he whisked distinguished visitors off to the site of the Majdanek concentration camp, to give them a 'preliminary taste' of Poland. Luckily I escaped that little excursion. I was to have no illusions – off to the chalkface of a 'hardship post' in Łódź. Like Conrad's Manager in *Heart of Darkness*, the man spread unease, which was perhaps an appropriate emotion as I set off.

What were my first impressions of Łódź? I arrived from Warsaw after dark. On the edge of the black road, and sometimes, horrifyingly, in the middle of it, were the zig-zagging drunks that are a traffic hazard all their own in Poland. (I once saw something resembling a body-bag on the side of the main Warsaw-Kraków motorway, evidently a casualty awaiting 'collection'.) Huge lorries with feeble headlights loomed past, lethal tractors with no tail-lights pulled out in front of me; and entering the city there was the new hazard of trams and tramlines. I felt like the boy in Belloc's *Cautionary Tales* who runs away on first encountering the Motor Car. I never got completely used to the tramlines, especially when they were concealed by ice and sludge, and often followed them, rather than the road, into pick-up points and sidings. My diary records the first glimpses of the city proper in slightly hysterical vein: 'A black, lightless city – Expressionist – Maserel or Murnau; looming tenement blocks trailing electric cables. The trams are ghost-lit, white flattened faces against the glass.' And in notes for a projected poem[5] I jotted down thumbnail descriptions: 'A gridwork of unimaginable extension – steam pouring from every vent and spigot.' As if to overheat my imagination still more, my second night in Łódź I drove out without a map, with the express intention of losing myself in the streets and vague arterials. I passed the huge neon sign – Telimena – named after Mickiewicz's aristocratic beauty in *Pan Tadeusz*, and now a textile firm; I ended up in a cul-de-sac in front of some locked factory gates.

The BC Docent's flat in Łódź was in the Ulica Narutowicza, 79 m 31. That flat! It deserves an essay on its own… I would hardly recognize it now, I suspect, since it was redecorated after I left, and became a fairly comfortable scholar's den, or so I heard. In which case my successor's talent for interior decoration is greater than mine. I would be hard put to imagine a more cheerless place, and my first act was to roll up a slime-green carpet and stash it in a corner. The curtains were of cheap textile with a garish design, hanging short of the sill (it is no accident that the first poem I taught my students at the Instytut was Larkin's 'Mr Bleaney'). The window-sills themselves were coated in a fine black grit, probably emanating from the power station I could see from the back window, along with the roofs of Łódź Fabryczna railway station. This grit seemed to penetrate sealed windows; it was my personal pollution gauge, just as other dwellings have a barometer on the wall. The bathroom was painted beige, with a dark brown lino floor, and the lavatory leaked, in a form of Chinese torture, from the overhead cistern. With its ugly furniture and hard rectangles, I never managed to tame the place. The bed had one of those weird East European eiderdowns on it: its cover had a large hole in the middle – so a blanket could be stuffed into it, as I learned later. As countless others must have done, I sat down on the bed, and like Bleaney, 'tried to shake off the dread'... I murmured the expat's prayer – 'Blessed be the World Service.' (Even Gorbachev said that, when he was cut off in his Crimean dacha during the failed coup of 1991.) I also spent inordinate amounts of time soaking in a hot tub, for of central heating and hot water there was no end.

There was a primitive TV set which I fiddled with for hours, succeeding only in obtaining various patterns of static; except for once, in mid-November, when I picked up a blurred image of Lech Wałęsa addressing a joint session of Congress. Sitting in that flat I transcribed his words, spoken in the Polish heroic tradition: 'There is no longer a question of dying for Gdańsk but of living for it... Poland's negotiated example can be held up as a model for other countries... But it doesn't come easy to Poland: in World War II her losses were the heaviest, her fight was the longest... And after the War, an alien form of government, alien economy, alien law, alien philosophy... Whatever Poland achieved she achieved through her obstinacy and relentlessness... Poland is returning to the tradition of religious

Stephen Romer

and European values... But her economy is on the verge of catastrophe... We are not asking for charity – but we'd like to see our country treated as a partner and a friend... The supply of words on the world market is plentiful – let deeds follow words now... And I promise you that your aid will not be wasted and will never be forgotten...'

Meanwhile in Łódź, the trams clattered past below my window, shedding blue sparks, at five and six and seven o'clock each morning; there were queues for milk and vodka and a few perished vegetables. But in the supermarket across the street – or 'spozywozy'[6] as the expats called it, in abject defeat before Polish consonantal clusters – they sold ham and sausage and tinned sardines and Russian Krim champagne, at wildly inflated prices. My colleague across the road, Irena Janicka Świderska, who was always touchingly concerned for my welfare, listed all the ten or so types of sausage, and gave me the good advice to buy up any novelty on the shelves, like bananas, for they might not be seen again. She had saved a bottle of French wine against my coming, and with her husband Bolesław, a true old-style Polish gentleman, we drank it one evening before Christmas. For the record, I jotted down some comparative prices, along with their sterling equivalent. This is how things stood on October 27, 1989: a ticket to the opera cost 750 złotys, or around 7p; a can of Heineken lager cost 8000zł, or 80p; a bottle of vodka, 2500zł, or 25p; a sirloin steak, 17000zł, £1.70; a pizza at the Hotel Polonia, 3000zł, 30p. The dollar was exchanging at 8000zł (premium rate), and the official rate (still in force at the time) fetched 2500zł. My Polish monthly salary was around £30, and as inflation rose payday at the University Rektorat almost required a Weimar-style barrow for the złoty notes, even though they were being printed in larger and larger denominations. For my last epic party I spent nearly a million złotys on beer, vodka and Russian champagne. I am proud to say, this one entered the annals of Instytut history.

Parties were the saving grace of those first months: the Poles have a genius for them. It was more or less expected of the BC Docent that he or she would give parties, but I was invited by students and staff alike to several. After my first fraught seminar (I spoke on Conrad for three hours solid, until one student summoned up the courage and asked me to stop), one of the girls came up and invited me to a party that evening: I have rarely felt so grateful to anyone. It was a pattern that continued, and since I was lucky enough to have a car, I would ferry staff and students around Łódź, the Renault resembling more and more a mobile igloo under its duvet of snow. The knack was to dodge the ubiquitous blue and white milicja vans by weaving round the side streets and avoiding the grand boulevards like Piotrkowska. Once, as bad luck would have it, I was stopped on the way home from a wedding reception, without my papers. The police wanted to take me 'down to the station', but while I sat in dismayed silence, the young Pole accompanying me negotiated a bribe over several cigarettes – the highest denomination dollar bill I had on me. I heard of a friend who, after drinking vodka too copiously, slumped unconscious over a bar table, and was taken down to something called 'the police shower room'[7]... We all drank and smoked heavily, but nothing compared to the Poles on payday evening. I would watch their comic choreography on the square in front of the opera house, an involved, weaving zigzag, interrupted by abrupt halts and sudden collapses in the snow.

Like any Westerner, I was shocked by the paucity of public watering holes; there was a dreadful kawiarnia (coffee house) almost opposite the flat, usually closed; there was the upmarket Dom Aktory opposite the opera; there was a seedy one-armed bandit joint called Maxims and a grim nightclub called the Kaskade housed in a concrete bunker. Often we assembled in the bar of the Grand Hotel on Piotrkowska, where a threadbare pianist would play schmaltz, and suspicious groups of black marketeers would engage in conspiratorial discussion. Western businessmen in their cups would bargain for the tarts lining the wall of the tiny cocktail bar. There was joy when a pizzeria opened in the Hotel Polonia, but such was the stench of cooking and stale parmesan in that overheated airless room that by the end of the year I could not go in without gagging. Once the entrance was barred because, as a friend put it, a drunk had parked a tiger over the carpet. By 1990 there was a rash of new bars and restaurants, including several Chinese places. We ate a peculiarly Polish version of Chow Mein in the Złoty Kaczka, or Golden Duck. The Pewex dollar shops (as they still were then) drew us like Aladdin's cave – 'a spillage of gold light on the sludge'... Here you could buy spirits, Western beer, decent French wine; in Polish bars a request for red wine could bring anything from a good Bulgarian Cabernet to Vermouth. There were also (strictly incorrect in the born-again Catholic Poland) German condoms on sale, with the brutally graphic brand-name of 'Anti-Baby', as if for added provocation. Sometimes, other consumable miracles arrived from nowhere to lighten up the day: I have a memory of baroque creamy-white curlicues of vanilla, that delicious Polish lody, being passed in cornets out of an improbable grimy hatchway that had opened suddenly on to the street. By the end of the year we had discovered Dworek, a first-class restaurant a little way into the birchwoods north of town. With its lawn and adjoining cottages, we could have been in the Cotswolds. Even then it must have been a haunt of the old Party nomenklatura, and of the new financial mafia (the two are often the same); there were Mercs and Porsches parked outside.

There are few things more intriguing than the changing iconography of a nation in the throes of radical political upheaval. The huge Coca-Cola billboard, masking the red state plaque of a former Party building says more than pages of political theorizing. The Marriott Hotel in Warsaw, that crystal fairyland of American capitalism, dwarfs the Palace of Culture, an example of Gotham City High Stalinist architecture, the dictator's 'gift to a grateful nation'. There is a bookshop inside the latter, where I found Czesław Miłosz's *The Captive Mind*, which would have been as significant for the Poles as finding Solzhenitsyn on open sale in Moscow for the Russians. By 1990, the martyred heroes of the first docker's strike figured in bronze, on the reredos of Sw. Brygidy in Gdańsk. In Częstochowa, on Easter Day, the scene at the tomb was acted out, and the Polish centurions carried shields embossed with the recrowned Polish eagle. After my return to the West, I read that *Animal Farm* and *1984* had become required reading on the state school syllabus.

It was, I suppose, inevitable that the Łódź Ghetto, and all the tragic events surrounding it, should have come to take a hold on my imagination. On my return to England, I wrote a series of poems about it[8], drawing on the material I had found in two remarkable books, *The Chronicle of the Łódź Ghetto* (1984) and

Łódź Ghetto (1989). The former book contained the text of the official Chronicle, liable to be read by the Gestapo, so it is a fascinating exercise in dissimulation, and all the horror is to be read between the lines. It contained reports like this, written without apparent irony: 'The construction of an exemplary road to the Cemetery has been in progress in Marysin for 3 weeks now. The building of exemplary roads under present conditions is a monument to the ghetto's vitality.' Or this, rather less deceived: 'In spite of such a horrendously large number of gravediggers, no more than 50 graves can be dug per day. The reason: a lack of skilled labour as well as – the *frozen ground*.' I deliberately chose All Souls' Night, when the Catholic cemeteries are ablaze with candles, to visit the ragged acres of the Jewish cemetery in Łódź. The Cmentarz Żydowski is one of the most haunting places imaginable. Fragments of headstones covered in dense Hebraic script litter the ground, lying untouched since the Nazis smashed them with sledgehammers. By feeble torchlight, we could make out the emblems: the small hands for a child, the flower, the broken tree, the books and the Ark of the Covenant. At one end of the Cemetery, against the wall which is now hung with memorial plaques to those who perished, set up by Jewish relatives, now in faraway America or Israel, there are some open pits. These were intended by the Nazis for the last group of Jewish gravediggers, but the Red Army arrived before they could carry out their last abomination. To this day, the pits have not been filled in. I have no wish to linger here on this subject, but one of the grimmest reminders that anti-Semitism is not dead in Poland occurred during the municipal elections in May, 1990. The posters of the WKO, one branch of fragmented Solidarność, were scrawled with the Star of David by a rival group on the far right.

No account of this kind would be complete without a description of at least one arrest. My own was rather spectacular. A journey to the Eastern frontier of the country, to see the famous bison and ancient oaks of Białowieża, ended with a night in Russia[9], in the custody of the Red Army. Inadvertently, we managed to pass the sleeping Polish frontier police and found ourselves peering through a high wire fence into Russia. What we did not know, and were soon to find out, was that we were already some fifty metres inside Russian territory. A military jeep drew up containing what I supposed were irate Polish soldiers; I swallowed hard when I saw the Hammer and Sickle on their berets. The unsmiling captain in charge told us to get in; as we were ferried off to the dacha of the border police, he took sadistic pleasure in releasing the safety catch on his rifle; then, as he went off to consult with his superiors, he left us under guard in the jeep, with the engine running, facing an endless road that led into Russia. The gravity of the situation only dawned slowly, but by that time I had dire presentiments and thought of the fate of Mathias Rust, the German aviator who had landed his plane in Red Square and was sentenced to four years detention. At that time, the USSR was still intact.

We were not put out of our misery when we got taken to the border guards hut and, locked in a room, awaited separate interrogation. We waited hours, while our Russian hosts alerted the Polish police. Through the window, as darkness fell, I could see a string of military vehicles arriving, apparently from both sides of the frontier. This was rapidly escalating into a minor international incident. Eventually a samovar was brought in, and we drank tea and ate biscuits. Then we were taken in turn to another room for interrogation. One of my companions was a friend from England, and I rather think it was her astonishing behaviour that saved the day. I could hear through the wall the following question: 'What would happen in England if you were caught at the border?' Olivia replied, 'I should think I would be sent back to where I had come from.' 'Do you know what the penalty for illegal entry into the Soviet Union is?' – 'No, I can't think.' – 'Four years imprisonment'. And then I heard a peal of laughter, and a gurgled 'You *wouldn't*!' By this time, I was feeling quite sick, and I couldn't believe my ears. She then regaled our captors with a description of her little boys waiting for her at Heathrow, who would be so disappointed if she didn't appear. I could only imagine their bemused faces.

Our 'trial', as they called it, continued. Our names and addresses were endlessly relayed by squawky radio to KGB headquarters, the quaint names of English villages transformed into bizarre exotic Russian syllables. They employed the usual theatrical gags to frighten us to death. My map had been confiscated on arrival; an officer came in with it, claiming to have found a cross in biro some way inside Russian territory, and demanding what it meant. There was indeed a cross, freshly printed in Russian ink... Our films were taken out and destroyed. The worst moment of all came when I was asked to hand over my car keys to the Polish police, evidently angry and humiliated by the situation. Had I been in lighter mood, I would have asked them to keep the engine ticking over, so I could recover it in four years time. And then, without warning, our 'interpreter' came in and announced that the trial was over. We had to write a formal letter of apology to the Soviet State, which he dictated to us in peculiar English. We then sat round drinking tea, while Olivia charmed the soldiers of the Red Army, promising to write a novel about them, and revisit them – this time, though, I chipped in hastily, from the right side of the border.

---

1 The overseas education department. (ed.)
2 Wajda's film *The Promised Land* depicts Łódź in the mid-19th century – days of rampant capitalism.
3 The Communist youth organisation. (ed.)
4 The British pop-singer, not the German Wagnerian composer. (ed.)
5 From his experience in Łódź and in particular his response to its no longer extant Jewish ghetto, Stephen Romer wrote a group of poems which he included in his collection *Plato's Ladder* (OUP, 1992); to it this essay might be read as a prose counterpart. (ed.)
6 The Polish word is spożywczy. (ed.)
7 See 'A Letter from Łódź' in this book, note to line 146. (ed.)
8 See note 5 above. (ed.)
9 In fact, what is now Belarus – though as late as this writing (1998), some Poles still refer to states which border theirs on the east and north-east as 'Russia'. (ed.)

George Hyde

Don's Return

Friday: Kraków via Paris, an odd route, to take up the post of visiting Professor of English at the ancient Jagiellonian University. The peculiar intimacies of Poland, 1992, have penetrated the austere plastic spaces of Charles de Gaulle airport. One man carries a pair of wheels, unmistakably wheelchair wheels, and another the time-honoured knobbly brown paper parcel. For a moment it looks as if we might be walking into Kantor's surreal theatre, but it turns out to be just an aging Russian jet, sporting stickers to the effect that LOT is now operating in conjunction with Air France. So what's new?

Saturday: Since the end of the Communist era Poland has indeed been engulfed with gratuitous information. Lamp-posts tell you where you can buy sex. The new map of Kraków tells you that it is new and has the 'new' (i.e. often the 'old') street names. The cabaret round the corner has a lurid new poster outside for a show called (I kid you not) 'Edward Penishands'. The new milk powder boasts (twice) of being imported. A Polish-made saucepan costs 70,000 złotys (about £3), while the 'new' imported kind is around 300,000. My professorial salary here for a month is less than £200. Poles are still moonlighting, rather more earnestly than before. There was a joke in the old days: 'They pretend to pay us, and we pretend to work.' It would be hard to demonstrate that things have got 'better': everyone seems to be working really hard, but the money is still pretty fictitious. The mood is tense. Grim stories pass around about new waves of attacks on Poles in Germany, and reprisals back home in Poland. The local Kraków paper has a depressing feature on one of the unemployed who tried very hard to set up a 'private' business, and failed miserably. In the old days, it was only the rats who raced. But there is, as they remind themselves, 'everything' in the shops, and I remember only too well those times, back in the '70s, when even Russian matches and the ubiquitous packets of biscuits ran out, never mind meat and cheese.

Sunday: Small wonder, then, that the traditional charm and hospitality of this perennially fascinating country, downfall of many a well-meaning young Englishman, has worn a bit thin, though people do still make an effort. Probably no one, not even Jerzy Urban (editor of the vitriolic opposition paper *Nie*) would want what people ironically call 'the good old days' back again. But there is a different spectre haunting Poland now: not the spectre of Communism, but the older and more familiar spectre of poverty, of deprivation, of envy; and academics are by no means immune. The man who kindly turned out to meet me at Kraków's funny little airport spoke bitterly of rising unemployment (14% in October 1992); and when we went together to a new pizza bar and there was no Polish beer, only Austrian, he took it out on the waitress (you are still allowed to do this in Poland) and then called the manager. At first I thought he was over-reacting. Now I'm not so sure; and when I do the shopping I find myself deliberately choosing only goods from the former Evil Empire (to borrow Reagan's colourful Hollywoodesque term), and not just because they're cheaper. The shops seem to be open almost all the time; the spirit of commerce has the whole country by the throat; this is the triumph of *détente*. It's not all bad; the centre of Kraków is filled with little stalls, and some Latin American folk musicians, with an admixture of Poles, are entertaining people on one side, while on the other someone is singing a jolly (and seemingly quite innocuous) song about the Pope.

Monday: Kraków is, of course, one of the wonders of European architecture, as the guide book keeps telling us. Yet it is still curiously low profile. Poles would rather grumble about the pollution from Nowa Huta than take pleasure in the beauty of their surroundings. Maybe they haven't time for such luxuries

George Hyde

and leave all that to the German tourists who are still, at the end of a long hot summer, much in evidence. Kraków's powerful Gothic piles, and peeling Renaissance stucco, speak of glories that are past; it isn't on the big trade routes, and the River Vistula is no longer of great commercial significance. The University, the 'Polish Oxford', is one of the oldest in the world; but every time the trumpeter plays from the tower of the Marian church, cutting short his call in memory of the Tartar arrow that felled his predecessor, Kraków reminds itself of Poland's irredeemably tragic history; and who cares, really? that's the problem.

Tuesday: Anyway, they've given me a fairly spacious, though terribly noisy, professorial flat and a light-ish timetable. Have to re-read *Tess* at great speed, marvelling once again at Hardy's creative way with melodrama, and how close he comes to telling the truth, the whole truth, about some of the naughty bits of Victorian mores, and then backs off – the 'good little Thomas Hardy', as Henry James called him (students always like that phrase). This quiet, sad, intelligent country, which erupts period-ically into wholly understandable violence, feels at home in Hardy's traumatised world. Poland has managed to sustain, through thick and thin, a good educational system, with lots of English teaching, surviving the Nazi occupation, Stalinism, and the stop-go of the reformed socialism that followed. Let's hope that consumerism will not undermine Poland's values, or the Church annex them. The world-wide retreat from education must inevitably threaten this dignified, traditional, independent institution as Communism never could. Looking out over the grey and silver and gold of an autumnal city preparing for a hard winter, you can't help wondering what the future holds. Are some people right to fear a 'czarna dyktatura', the black dictatorship of the clerisy? The priests are very much in evidence. But now that the Free World has given the Poles real incentives, real wealth, and real unemployment, which must surely take people's minds off matters of principle, will the Church not fade away? and with it, all those 'moral' problems? Not so: in the course of the academic year there is a terrible furore about abortion. When I was in Poland under the Communists, sex was the national sport (Poland has far more than her fair share of beautiful women, what's more). Now there are all the usual disturbing signs of commercial exploitation, Catholic backlash, and the old mix of self-righteousness and resentment preparing the way for a militant feminism of the kind Poland has never shown any interest in (perhaps because they love the sex war so much). 'Poveri noi', as D. H. Lawrence remarked.

Wednesday: Meet some students for the first time, in the University lobby. A rather cold stare: foreigners used to attribute this to Communism, but I think it is just an understandable habit of looking a gift horse in the mouth. And if the crowds don't look less glum than they did under Communism, it just isn't a Polish habit to smile and be pleasant for no reason, the way the Brits do, following the example of their American cousins – though you can see from the telly that the compulsion to smile is growing. I give my lecture on *Tess*, which virtually no one has read (one student has seen the film); Hardy's problems with sex and religion seem (unsurprisingly) to strike a chord. Afterwards, I have my 'office hours': do come and see me, I say, if you'd like to discuss your work. 'Maybe some other time', one girl says pertly, in faultless English. She's probably rushing off to give the well-paid private lessons which will support her studies.

Thursday: The library is a mixture of dusty cloth-bound tomes of uncertain age (are there some treasures here?[1]) and bright paper-backs in multiple copies supplied by my predecessor, courtesy of the British Council. The British Council has played an enormous-ly important role in Poland; under Kissinger's totally successful policy of *détente*, Poland was Numero Uno for subversion (the phrase chosen by a senior Council official in conversation with me). Poles used to rave on about how naïve we Brits were in being nice to the Russians: about how it would be our turn next, when the tanks rolled: but of course the policy of opening the frontiers each way, rather than patrolling them with massive hardware, could only work to the advantage of the West. Glossy consumer images (of which I was one, of course) ended the Cold War much faster than confrontation could ever have done. My BC predecessor's taste was impeccable, in a slightly Malcolm Bradbury/Booker Prize sort of way, and I grab an armful of recent novels I ought to have read – and find time to read them, which I could not do at my home university. The library borrower's slip asks a fearful lot of questions twice over in Polish, but I cope; after all, in the '70s we were a bilingual family[2]! And everyone is so nice! not all the time, especially to one another, where the Polish love of game-playing still rules. But despite the frequent histrionics, these Poles are no match for the British in aggression; and they are always so taken aback to find us one move ahead in the power stakes! They seem fated to box themselves into a corner, sooner or later, and then ritually to shoot themselves in the foot.

Friday: Stroll through the glowing classical streets to the massive Austrian-style administrative building. Great gaunt offices up marble staircases behind padded doors, with formidable secretaries adjusting imposing hairdos just like in Andrew Davies' clever television drama, *A Very Polish Practice*, which was partly shot here. One office per form: it elevates the mind, pacing up and down these magnificent landings. Finally I find my sought-after piece of paper: a contract, but I put off signing it until next week... I have taken advice from old friends, and think they are trying to get me too cheap.

Saturday: Breakfast off a tin of Estonian horse-mackerel which weighs (the label says) eight and four-fifths ounces. Honestly, I thought they were sardines... Been here a whole week; as another British Council lecturer (a contributor to this volume) said to me, days on end can pass here in a kind of swoon... like the fluid, deliquescent time-moods of Bruno Schulz, Poland's great Jewish writer of short stories, whose *The Street of Crocodiles* ran at the Cottesloe in a lovely production/adaptation by Théâtre de Complicité.

Back in 1976, Lublin felt so far away from eveywhere, its Jewish traditions seemingly irrevocably swept away by the Nazis, its Catholic University precariously hanging on to an intellectual world in touch with new Western developments. Now it had come slowly and painfully back to life. But the condition of 'normality' is probably the hardest for Poles to live with. A friend once said to me of the pre-War Polish republic, that it was 'a short holiday' – from the constraints of history, that is. In the early '90s in Kraków, there was an uncomfortable feeling in the air that what we were witnessing then could only be temporary, accompanied by the knowledge that the amazing creative outpourings of the Communist era would probably never be repeated.

---

[1] See Frank Tuohy's account of discovering, among other 'treasures', two manuscripts by Coleridge. (ed.)

[2] See Hyde's previous essay in this book. (ed.)

Cathal McCabe

A Letter from Łódź

(for Adam Wattam)

I tu mi serce na wieczność skradł
Ktos cichy i modro-złocisty,
I tu przez siedem ogromnych lat
Pisałem wiersze i listy.
  - *Julian Tuwim, 'Łódź'*

Adam, now 'seven enormous years'
– As Tuwim, local laureate,
Puts it in this early verse –
Into what I think of yet
As a kind of afterlife, this hand-
Shake from The Promised Land.

Thus, po-faced on a million note,
Reymont dubbed the mile on mile
Of chimney stacks – each cotton-
Crazed satanic mill   10
Coughing up each endless night
Here in 'Poland's Manchester', Tuwim's town

Of 'smoke and grime'.
Now no proud production-talk
Or promises. A heaving, discontented hulk
With no tradition, legend, myth,
No ancestry, no noble birth,
With neither style, nor sense, nor charm,

A vegetating paradox:
A settlement of chimneys, mud,   20
Of palaces and wooden shacks,
Of fortunes and of penury,
Of hunger – and of greed;
Of boredom, dirt, brutality –

This *is our inheritance.*
Where workers' children's rain-
Bows were the coloured dyes that ran
From paintworks through the gutters
And down the stinking drains –
Like the fortunes that were squandered, frittered   30

Fast away, by the one-time Lodzer millionaires,
The Grohmanns, Grynbergs, Geyers,
Who disappeared in wreaths of smoke
And left our wretched 'Boat' unmanned,
A millstone round the neck
Of an agricultural land.

– So Tuwim wrote, between the wars.
Astonished at the dirt and dark
(In which he grew up happily)
He yet would write, in later years   40
(To Sztaudynger on Żwirki
Street): *You know, I miss Łódź desperately.*

Cathal McCabe

Do końca będę pięknie kłamać,
Obyz się tylko nie załamać...
When you rented a room
From Sztaudynger's daughter
And sat with a half, or quarter,
Litre, bent to a candle in the gloom,

You set aside his 'beautiful lies',
Set to recording the luckless lives   50
And souls in distress
In this desperate place,
The city he couldn't help but translate,
Your Englishman in Łódź. In *Boat.*

If ever there was a misnomer
This has got to be it:
No sea, no lake, no water-
Fall. Just the Łódka, hard to find,
A fetid, futile, underground
Source that's breathing yet.   60

Passing Piękna – Beautiful! – Street
The other day, I walked awhile
In the little wooded cemetery
Gasping by the pitted wall
Shuddering though standing yet
In spite of the daily battery

Of traffic thundering past.
Past streamers of steam
From vents and drains
And fumes from every foul exhaust   70
A leisurely tram
Skirts the purring power station's

Red-and-white-striped chimney stacks,
A banneret of dark
Grey smoke, the ragged oasis of a park...
An apolitical misery stalks
The central subway where there begs
A man with neither home nor legs.

Unearthly women still parade
Łódź's only boulevard   80
To speak of. In thigh-length boots
And bum-length skirts
They boldly pass
Each beggar in his appointed place.

On Płac Wolności – Freedom Square –
The same old guy
Still sets out his wretched wares:
Old, broken, faded toys
Litter an ancient canvas sheet
At his unconcerned, businesslike feet.   90

And still 'the stupid foreigners'
That Joyce observed in Rome
Keep on with their 'courageous
Attempts to pronounce the name
Of the street' or the dorm or the house
In which they have lived for years.

Sheltering from a shower of sleet,
Huddled in a dank, chill bar,
Its standard garden furniture
And then the inane patter and beat   100
Of one of the infant radio stations
Proof of our hard-won independence,

I watch young men with fiery skin
Down the suddy beer in one,
Then light up, knowing they were meant
For afterlives of unemployment.
Why celebrate in this dead town
An eagle given back his crown?

Where frozen actors, out of work,
Are showing drivers where to park;   110
Where salesgirls, work to do, complain
('This capitalistic carry-on!');
A barber, tea-break overdue,
Is glad to see the back of you.

Whatever are we now to *do*
In this, our 'new reality'? Walk
Along Piotrkowska Street, gawk-
Ing at the loud displays
Where light bulbs and compu-
Ters sit with jeans and deodorant sprays   120

(I remember it as a grim, dark stretch
With little more than a neon
Or two)? Jump the pudd-
Les? Dodge the mud?
Pass a wintry afternoon
Watching a hopeless football match?

Launch a fragile paper boat
Onto a stercoraceous pond?
Observe a passing pant-
Ograph's (still-surprising) lightning-bolt?   130
The dark descend, the silent snow
Streaming from the lamps below?

Yet walking now through bad Bałuty
I see – not fear and grime – but beauty:
After a smashing thunderstorm
I'm caught in the transcendental gleam
Of a yard off Łagiewnicka Street (astonished still
That I'm here at all).

Breakfast-, lunch- and tea-time-drunks
Cling to bus stops, walls and gates: 140
I watch as one negotiates
A gaping hole, a clanging tram; another weaves
Between the cars. (If any get home it's only thanks
To their skinny, ghost-grey, wandering wives.)

I picture them lying senseless in
A cell of the Izba Wytrzeźwień –
Urinous, damp, a judas-hole
Onto a row of belts on a wall,
The window barred, no light in use –
Hearing the rain, a moan, a curse.   150

The despair that is Commun-
Ism has few more telling
Symbols than the qual-
Ity of its beer- and spirit-labelling.
The beautiful bottle a common-
Place now, we wander the promise and col-

Our of supermarket, stall and bar.
And could it be that, *Judenrein,*
Sprayed a uniform, socialist grey,
Tense with longing, a city will pine   160
For a method, a tribe, that has passed away?
Is it nothing more than *marketeenk*, this run on beer

Cathal McCabe

And glittering vodkas rabbis from the east
Are daily sipping, stamping *kosher*
(Here in Łódź they no longer exist)?
Kosher beer, kosher porter,
Kosher orange squash – there
Is even kosher water!

Remember the cherished collections
Of German, French and Danish   170
Beer and soft drink cans,
A part once of any fashionable
Teenager's bedroom's furnish-
Ings, ranged on shelf and sill and table?

A cent-scavenging, Communist
Childhood now a thing of the past,
They watch as workmen lay the floor
Of what new throbbing restaurant,
What new plastic bar
(Every time you turn around   180

Another venture closes down,
Another tries its luck). There yet remain
– Though for how long? –
The milk bars' hidden poign-
Ancy: salt in an empty yoghurt carton,
A tablecloth's washable fruitbowl pattern.

If you change the name
Do you change the thing?
Do we lose or find our monotonous way
Through the chessboard centre's tired array   190
Of traitor-streets all at once become
Thoroughfares fit for general, king,

Cardinal, saint and partisan?
(Their crumbling tenements crumble on.)
Does picking the first two letters off
(I've seen this done) police car doors
All of a sudden make bobbies of
A truly efficient, unprincipled force?

Why *are* policemen policemen?
Because they R, U C.   200
The oldest joke again falls flat
In a 'British Culture' semin-
Ar – though I am already
Miles away, gloomily reflecting that

The UB, SB – as you like –
Were there to hold the world in check;
ZOMO moonmen meant to beat
Some sense into the non-élite;
We know the cruising ORMO van
No early-morning sliced or pan.   210

I think of a beaten, bitter friend
Making the most of a makeshift end,
Obliged to work with those who will
Not now be made accountable.
To think that those who caused his scars
Are driving free in costly cars.

While I sit on my privileged arse
Seven floors up in the night
And gaze blankly across
At each imagined life – its light: 220
The soul-glow of a TV set,
The mortuary-glare of a kitchenette.

The tame illuminations
Of a square, socialist block;
The changing, pleasing permutations
Till after ten – or eleven – o'clock
(The stairwells alone
Stay lit till dawn).

Somnambulant workmen
Weld the tracks   230
Trams have pounded through the day;
Swinging lanterns, spilling sparks
(Minds no doubt on double-pay)
They sweat beneath a blazing moon.

Then there's the man in the family
Welding a wieldy satellite dish
Onto their tiny balcony,
His spluttering heroics
A symbol of our consummate wish
For *European* atmospherics: 240

With our D.I.Y. we are soldiering on.
I think of Ireland in twenty-two, hear
Above the buzz of the Sejm
(Its cast and blather ever the same):
*Poland shall get Her
Freedom, and you still solder on.*

So were you now to ask me,
Say, when Mazowiecki's government fell
Or when Wałęsa fought it out,
Publicly and desperately,   250
With the dangerous Tymiński – well,
I'd find it hard to give the date.

I could however tell you when
The brash, exotic beers
And fruits, and Argentinian wine,
Snug in dollar-shop displays,
Ceased to brandish dollar-signs – those mythical days!
And the black marketeers

In their denim suits – as if
Rounded up and herded off   260
To some distant death camp
Only the mad
Could even begin to contemp-
Late – suddenly disappeared.

This week fifty years ago
A further, frantic search began
For those who would indeed be sent
'To work in the Generalgouvernement',
Finish up in Buchenwald. In the Beginning
Was the Ghetto.   270

Rumkowski is the elder Yeats
– White mane
And monocle – out among
The waifs and strays
(Schoolchildren, as he says).
A public man, he now berates

A workforce that can barely stand,
Cries, 'Only work
Can save us from the worst!'
Then, 'Jews of the Ghetto, understand: 280
These soup strikes are a waste
Of time. Have you gone berserk,

Thinking I can thicken soup?!'
Tall as the spires on Zgierska Street,
He watches ov-
Er his sick domain, this, and every other, night:
'If I told them *half* of what I know
They would not sleep.'

Before the church's dark facade
A plaster Virgin now stands guard.   290
An aisling in the sodium light
She lifts her eyes to heaven,
The clocks still stopped at ten to eight,
Five minutes past eleven.

She won't have heard,
A mile away, the hurried
Executions, shaking the Jewish Cemetery;
The regular gunfire over the pits; each
Bullet's mad finality –
One for a young Różewicz.   300

Underneath a leaden sky
A woodpecker pounds
A leafless tree (early March in Łódź),
Today the only other sounds
The crackling of the rain – and then my
Swishing through the weeds,

Over the brown, sodden leaves
Stuck to paths, in grass, on graves;
Past mausoleum, modest plaque,
Along a narrow cinder track...   310
Against a tree, tall as a man,
A headstone leans and weeps, in the rain.

As those who wept in the blinding light
Flooding their cellar, or their pit. Emac-
Iated, dying still, amazed
Survivors clamber out...
A matter of yards from where I sit
They run down Franciszkańska Street.

And fifty years ago this spring
The Eldest of the Jews   320
Had 'his' force surrendering
Any music left in them. Priceless cellos,
Violins; lutes and flutes; a saxophone;
Sold to the city for saccharine.

While Łódź's greatest (Jewish) sons
(And two of *Europe*'s best musicians),
Tansman, and then Rubinstein,
Far from the hell of Litzmannstadt,
Concerted, suppered, swam and sat
Out of the Hollywood sunshine.   330

When, his tiresome law course done,
Gombrowicz first discovered the South –
A heady mix of oranges, wine,
The warmth and glare of a liberal sun,
The light, the air, the youth
To whom he took a shine –

He spoke of his 'joy', 'relief'
And 'hope' – and then of how
His 'later life'
Could only opt for the permanent sun   340
Of somewhere like the Argentine.
Hłasko, 'wild, objectionable' (Dąbrow-

Cathal McCabe

Ska's words in praising him!) snapped:
'I'm off in a year or two – and nev-
Er coming back' – Our daily dream, in which we wake
In freezing, starless, first-tram dark
– *Cité pleine de rêves* –
To find we have (like you) escaped...

So while – at least to my fanciful eye –
Palms explode in the bluest sky   350
Beyond your newly-whitewashed door,
Here, as you know, all's little more
Than a spectrum, a trauma, of varying greys:
The sky, the will, the holidays.

Yet look down on the roads below:
In multi-coloured coats and caps
Children from a nearby school
Clutching catkin wands and maps
Scour allotments flecked with snow
To find a leaf, a daffodil: 360

An eager, earnest *Search for Spring* –
The yearly theme come round again.
And Spring, who never lets us down,
Releases dazzled boy-recruits
Who, drunk on freedom, roam the streets
In blazing shawls, who sway and sing

(You think at first of soccer thugs);
Releases carpets, mats and rugs,
Hauled out into public view
And soundly beaten, black and blue;   370
And, last of all, injects the trees
That stretch now in the dirty breeze.

For Nature, like a teenage crush
– Obsessive, inexplicable –
Refuses to abandon us. So, chisell-
Ing at weathered loaves,
Swallow, sparrow, wren and thrush
Build (Come build!) in breeze-block eaves

And pigeons skid and clatter
On every narrow sill;   380
A rooster, from what depths, what plot or
Square of tended mud,
Ignoring block to right and left, sends abroad
Its raucous, unexpected call.

Łódź, 'the strangest place on earth',
Will waken of her own accord –
Her beat-up winos, haggard
Whores, suit-and-sneakers *biznes*men,
Crimson-jacketed 'entrepreneurs';
Her giant moon   390

And astrology; her burge-
Oning churches, flea-pit bars,
Wretched Russians, wild bazaars;
Her rows of in-
Fants, red with rage.
– The strangest place! Where I live on,

Here in Tuwim's 'brud i dym',
Among the ghosts of suicides
And those who knew but one shrill song
Before the dead-end firing-squads   400
And now the yuppies and the young
Who don't give a damn.

March-June 1994

Notes

The poem was first published in a collectors' edition by *Correspondance des Arts*, Łódź, 1996.

2   *Julian Tuwim* (1894-1953). The essays drawn on here, *My Childhood in Łódź* (1925) and *Memories of Łódź* (1934), are collected in *Prose Writings*. In the former, Tuwim speaks of Łódź as 'the most bizarre city on earth'.

8   *Władysław Reymont* (1867-1925). Nobel Prize winner and author of *Ziemia obiecana (The Promised Land)*, a novel set in Łódź at the end of the last century. The city's great textile industry had led to it being called The Polish Manchester.

41   *Jan Izydor Sztaudynger* (1904-1970). Writer of satirical verse and epigrams, with whom Tuwim corresponded in the years 1946-53 while Sztaudynger was living in Łódź. The epigram cited might be rendered: 'Beautifully will I lie to the end:/May I not go round the bend!'

54   *Boat*. 'Łódź' in Polish, and the title of Adam Wattam's second novel (Biblioteka, Łódź, 1997), in which the protagonist, an Englishman, lives on Piękna Street.

81   *Łódź's only boulevard/To speak of*. Piotrkowska Street, described by one guidebook as 'probably the best known street in Poland'.

133   *Bałuty*. Area to the north of the city, traditionally synonymous with poverty and crime. It was here, in the oldest and most impoverished part of Łódź, that the Nazis established the ghetto in 1940.

146   *Izba Wytrźewień*. Lock-up for drunks. Literally, 'sobering-up station'.

152   *The despair that is Communism*. Quoted from *Boat*.

162   *Marketing*. Among those words (chiefly concerned with business and catering) which Polish has taken from English in recent years. (When the final g is devoiced, the Polish speaker will say *marketeenk*.)

191   *Traitor-streets*. Since the political changes in 1989-90, many street-names have (again) been changed, so that, for example, *Red Army* is now *Piłsudski* Avenue, *Dzierżyński* now *Home Army* Street, *Allende* now *Popiełuszko* Street, and so on. Practically all of the street-names Tuwim listed in 1934 as reflecting the character of the city – 'Weaver's St, Factory St, Storage St, Spinning St, Goods St, Industrial St, Canal St, Lime St, Deaf St, Dark St, Empty St, Cemetery St... and Beggar's Lane' – remain to this day. The Polish police – *Milicja* (Militia) – was renamed *Policja* in 1990.

205   *UB, SB*. Urząd Bezpieczeństwa (Department of Security) and Służba Bezpieczeństwa (Security Service), former names for the Polish Security Police.

207   *ZOMO*. Zmotoryzowane Oddziały Milicji Obywatelskiej (Riot Squad).

209   *ORMO*. Ochotnicza Rezerwa Milicji Obywatelskiej ([Voluntary] Police Reservists). In Northern Ireland, Ormo Bakery vans delivered fresh bread daily.

243   *Sejm*. The Polish Parliament.

246   *Poland shall get Her/ Freedom...* Yeats, 'Parnell': 'Parnell came down the road, he said to a cheering man:/ "Ireland shall get her freedom and you still break stone."'

270   *In the Beginning/ Was the Ghetto*. The phrase occurs in the notebooks of Oskar Rosenfeld, first published in *Łódź Ghetto*, edited and compiled by Alan Adelson and Robert Lapides (Viking, 1989). He was deported to the Łódź Ghetto from Prague in October 1941, where he worked in the Ghetto Archives and wrote for the Ghetto *Chronicle*. He left with one of

the last deportations to Auschwitz during the liquidation of the Ghetto in August 1944. The same fate awaited Mordechai Chaim Rumkowski who, after the German occupation of Łódź – renamed Litzmannstadt, after the First World War general Karl Litzmann who fell near the city – became Chairman of the Jewish Council of Elders. With the establishment of the Ghetto, Rumkowski became its virtual ruler, with responsibility for and power over all aspects of life in the Ghetto's four square kilometres, housing in 1941 163,777 people, in 1944 – 877.

300 *A young Różewicz.* Janusz, elder brother of the poet Tadeusz, executed on 21 October 1944. The much-anthologized poem, 'The Survivor', written at the end of the war, begins, 'I am twenty-four/led to slaughter/ I survived.'

318 *They run down Franciszkańska Street.* From Jakub Poznański's account of his family's liberation in January 1945 in his *Diary from the Łódź Ghetto* (*Pamietnik z getta łódzkiego*, Łódź, 1960), a fragment included in *Łódź Ghetto.*

327 *Aleksander Tansman* (1897-1986). Composer. Like *Artur Rubinstein* (1887-1982), he left Łódź at an early age, spending most of his life abroad.

332 *Witold Gombrowicz* (1904-1969) and *Marek Hłasko* (1934-1969). Leading Polish 20th century novelists, both exiles for much of their lives. The novelist *Maria Dąbrowska* (1889-1965) came to Hłasko's defence after a campaign against him in the State press in the late 1950s.

Emma Harris

Afterword

The last British Council literature lecturer left Poland in 1998. Throughout the 1990s, the Council had been slowly edging its resources away from English Studies in university departments and switching to brighter, market-oriented areas, where it was thought that the returns would be more crudely immediate. Support was focused on the training of teachers of English in newly-established colleges with a three-year 'Licencjat' degree programme, and on promoting 'British Studies', that mish-mash of cultural studies and sociology which was supposed to open up markets for British pop music and language textbooks. English departments had to compete for funds for 'links' and 'projects', some of which have undoubtedly been highly successful and beneficial; but the universities' special place in Council concerns, cemented for 40 years through the presence of a British lecturer, quietly vanished. The organisation's headquarters building in Aleje Jerozolimskie (variously and nostalgically described in this volume as 'quaint', 'old-fashioned' and 'reassuring') still contains a library, but much of the space is now given over to language classrooms, and the ground floor has become a tourist information centre, run jointly with the British Tourist Authority. Gone are the days when British lecturers could pull a sizeable audience for 'Shakespeare's Sonnets' or a series on 'English monarchs'. The lecture hall itself is gone; occasional visiting poets can be squeezed into the largest classroom, but if some bigger name is wheeled out for a special event (like John le Carré in 1998), suites have to be hired in hotels. Up and down the staircase tramp Polish managers and civil servants, to receive instruction in 'business English', the *lingua franca* of the modern world.

In a way, things have come full circle. In 1939, Denis Hills was teaching English language courses at the Anglo-Polish School in Warsaw, while Egerton Sykes, the first British Council representative, doubled as an agent for patent bicycle saddles. People wanted to learn English, Hills tells us, 'to improve their pay and chances of promotion' in those last days before the War. 'Literature lecturers' were unheard of. Now, sixty years later, they have been and gone; this volume therefore marks the end of an era. Inevitably one is tempted to sum up, to ponder on the lecturers' role, on what they brought to Poland and on what Poland gave to them, and to consider – at a time when Poland trembles on the threshold of 'going into Europe' – what part they played in inter-cultural understanding. We might also consider, at a time when Poland has recently joined NATO, the part they played in what I believe is called cultural diplomacy – for undoubtedly in the understated British way that prevailed until the 1980s, they were intended to put an indirect spoke in the Communist wheel. They were, as George Hyde points out, sent out to Poland as instruments of the policy of *détente*.

I have perhaps been asked to write this afterword because I am thought to straddle the Polish-British cultural divide. This needs to be explained. In a way, over the past thirty years, I have moved – insofar as this is ever possible, perhaps really I'm just impaled – from one side of the cultural fence to the other. I came to Poland in 1968 on a twelve-month Polish government exchange scholarship, for which the British Council did the selection and provided the back-up. In some respects, I was in a better position to deal with the initial culture shock than most of the lecturers represented here. I could at least read Polish (although my first attempts to communicate orally – with a porter on the station in Kraków – showed that I still had a long way to go). On paper, I knew quite a lot about Polish history, and something about contemporary Poland. I had watched all the Polish films that the Edinburgh film theatre could provide. I had also acquired a distorted view of contemporary Polish politics by struggling through *Dziennik Polski*, the émigré paper, as an aid to everyday language learning. I was attached to the Jagiellonian University History Department, where no-one took much notice of me, and where I was not weighed down by my perceived cultural heritage. I was at a natural linguistic and academic disadvantage, rather than the other way round, which was probably good for my soul and grip on reality.

In those early days, the English Department in Kraków sought me out, but I had little opportunity of being lionized. At the same time, many of the snapshot views that I can recall from this early period chime with those recorded by the first writers in this volume. How well I remember the snow of that first winter: fairy-tale, snow-laden fir forests from the windows of an early morning train (5.10 a.m., that was certainly a cultural shock) to Warsaw; mad flurries of snowballing in the area around the student hostels; my life – I now believe – being saved by a bear-like figure in a padded jacket, who hurled me to the ground as I heedlessly walked down a pavement in Kraków just as several tons of snow were to be tipped off high roofs. Later, I moved to Warsaw, and by 1974 was myself employed in a university English department. My situation was still very different from that of a Council lecturer. I was still at an academic disadvantage: I had no qualifications in English Studies, and remain to this day alarmingly ignorant of much of what goes on in my own Institute, particularly in the field of linguistics. Luckily, after 1968, the Warsaw Institute had opened a Cultural Studies section, and as an economic historian I was not quite so far out of place there. I began to teach British social history, and gradually to find out more about what my colleagues in an English department actually did.

My initial ignorance disposed me to a curiosity that I find missing in many of the essays in this volume. Unlike most of the lecturers, I had contacts with other departments of the University, and with a growing circle of friends from other walks of life. And my financial situation was quite different from that of the lecturers. *Świadomość kształci byt* – consciousness is shaped by material circumstances, as the Marxists say. This was perhaps above all the factor that pushed me up and over the cultural barrier. Like everyone else, I had to struggle to make ends meet. Like everyone else, I felt the subtle financial divide that cut Council lecturers off from the rest of us. Increasingly I became part of the institution, a permanent fixture, rather than a bird of passage. Even after the thaw, there were not very many

English departments in Poland, given the size of the country – only eight full-blown ones until the 1980s, then ten – thus it was a cozy, family world in which everyone knew each another; and as a permanent fixture, I got to know a great many of the Council lecturers personally.

The essays in this volume are by a small and unrepresentative sample of Englishmen (with only an occasional woman) doing an unusual job in an unusual setting. They paint a startlingly uniform picture of Poland, Polish society, Polish universities and Polish colleagues in the Communist and immediately post-Communist period. In many ways they tell us more about the British, and British attitudes, than about Poland itself. What the lecturers saw is, of course, interesting in its own right, being in most cases a record of the 'naïf informant', as the linguists call him. But here a word of caution. How easily basic preconceptions can change what we see. I hate to take issue with so distinguished an observer as Derwent May, but both he and Stephen Romer are mistaken in claiming that in the early 1990s the Soviet-built Palace of Culture in Warsaw was dwarfed by the Marriott Hotel. This is simply not true. The Palace of Culture, when measured with protractors and measuring rods rather than the eye of the mind, remained the highest building in Warsaw until in 1998 it was topped by a few metres by a Korean-erected office block in distant Wola. What May and Romer saw was what they expected: the triumph of American capitalism – and what better symbol for this than the businessman's luxury hotel, owned by a U.S. chain, which after 1989 quite simply had to be taller than the people's palace built by the Soviets in a discredited era.

I am able to believe that this is what they really saw, rather than a consciously-constructed metaphor, because three years ago I visited Berlin for the first time since the Wall came down. I left in a hurry, with no time to check a map, and I couldn't remember whether Tegel airport was in the former West or East Berlin, but I had a feeling that it was in the old East. (Travel to Berlin before the Wall came down had always been beset with confusion, from the moment when the Interflug plane did a vertical take-off at Warsaw airport, to the moment when you emerged from the clutches of the hands-on East German customs officials; I had therefore evidently suppressed the names of airports.) On the way from the airport to the hotel, I looked out of the taxi windows and saw square, brick apartment blocks of the kind built everywhere in Eastern Europe in the 1950s; the few shops looked unappetising, and the population drab. Aha, I thought, despite German unification, you can still tell that this is East Berlin. When I arrived at the hotel, there was a plastic reception desk in high 1960s people's democratic style, and the bathroom in my room was covered with those tiny pale blue tiles that were so popular in Polish hotel bathrooms through the '60s and '70s. This was clearly an East Berlin hotel that had been privatised and smartened up a bit. But of course, it wasn't. When I finally looked at I map, I found that all the time I had been in the old West Berlin, driving through red Wedding to the centre.

I am not claiming that all of the patterns of remembrance that emerge in these accounts are constructs of the mind. But there is a remarkable schematicism about many of them. Shabbiness, shortage of space, the contrast between public and private, the mores of shopping, queues for taxis, queues for anything, and the human spirit transcending it all – these are the things observed and noted. (It's odd, incidentally, how so many of the negative phenomena have transferred themselves to Britain in the last decade of the 20th century.) Such details aside, what emerges above all is the love affair that developed between the lecturers and their host country, a strange, special-interest affair that often lasted life long.

What was it all about?

I see several basic ingredients in the spell that Poland cast over the lecturers. One was undoubtedly the ignorance with which the majority of them landed at their destination. Apart from basic pre-conceptions, taken as a whole, they did not on arrival know much about the culture they were entering. This is not surprising. Despite two World Wars fought over Eastern Europe, it has seldom played much part in the British scheme of things. There had been a small 19th century Polish émigré group in Britain, which had made little impact, and Poland's liberation struggles never attracted the same attention as, for example, those of Kossuth and the Hungarians. Some works of Polish literature were translated into English, and a little specialist interest was taken in Polish history, although the *liberum veto* was about the only item that had entered the canon. Contacts between Britain and Poland had not been well developed before the War, and the late treaty obligation was something on paper, rather than in flesh and blood. A few eccentric Englishmen – like Commander Edward Hilton Young, who, after losing an arm in the First World War, and taking part in a variety of missions to Russia and Poland, had received an estate in Poland's eastern marches from his friend Count Radziwiłł, and was shooting duck there when the Second World War broke out; he swam one-armed across the Baltic to reach neutral territory and return to Britain – had fallen in love with Poland in the early 20th century, and had written about it[1]. During the War, there had been a bit more information, at the level of war reporting and Allied propaganda: Polish pilots in the Battle of Britain; Sikorski at Gibraltar; Poles at Monte Cassino; the Warsaw Uprising. But then the Iron Curtain came down, and news was restricted.

As the War receded into the distance, and the Iron Curtain dug itself in deeper, real news of Poland became ever thinner in Britain. A few people saw Wajda's films, a few people had heard of Grotowski and Kantor. But ideas about Poles did not form part of the popular consciousness. If the lecturers were given any information before they left, it was mainly irrelevant and out of date, and generally of the Cold War variety. I can add to the tales told in these essays: I remember as a scholarship holder in the late 1960s being taken into a basement in some outpost of the Foreign Office and shown a two-way mirror. This, we were told, would undoubtedly feature in the accommodation provided for us by Polish universities, and the thing to do was hang a towel over it. Inevitably, when we finally reached the Dom Studentek 'Jadwiga', our student hostel in Kraków, there were no mirrors at all. By the 1980s, this kind of thing had apparently been replaced by practical hints on day-to-day survival, conveyed out of context. I am amazed by Stephen Romer's revelation that the Council in 1989 was advising 'the vital necessity of equipping oneself with an all-purpose bath plug'. Clearly none of the recipients of this advice took any notice: the number of bath plugs that I have supplied over the years to wailing Council visitors would fill a small Dunlop re-processing plant.

And so the lecturers were parachuted half-blind into a new context, and fumbled to gain a foothold. This naturally heightened their sensibilities and helped to shape the extraordinarily strong impression that Poland and the Poles made upon them. Moreover, the lecturers came from a country in which nothing ever seemed to happen or to have happened. In the 1950s, it is true, memories of war were recent: uncles had been killed on distant battlefields, London and Coventry had seen the blitz, there had been ration cards, a black market, a home guard. But after that, it had all been National Health orange juice, school milk, consensus politics and passing exams. And the lecturers were coming to a country where too many things had happened, and were still happening. This was in the air, screened and mysterious, in the '50s, '60s and '70s, and came out into the open in a somewhat vulgar form in the 1980s.

Nor could the things happening be entirely deciphered. The language barrier helped here. Very few of the lecturers learned Polish; some tried and did not get far; some acquired only what they called 'restaurant Polish'. All were discouraged from and despised for doing it by their native colleagues. Staff in English departments who had invested too much in acquiring the high-status English language gaped in feigned or genuine incomprehension whenever one of these outsiders attempted to communicate in the tongue of the country. But the impenetrability of the language fostered magic. The metaphors and idioms of communication, translated into the English of their colleagues and students, which was the medium through which almost all of the lecturers saw the Polish world, had the charm of novelty. I remember the delight with which thirty years ago I took the hoary old Polish joke, 'They pretend to pay us and we pretend to work' as an example of the wit and originality of a new acquaintance of mine – and the scorn with which my enthusiasm was received when I repeated it. (Much as an American friend once enthused about my use of language when I wrote to her about someone or other, 'All their geese are swans').

Then there was that certain wild bohemianism about Poland, the intimacy afforded by underprivilege among the intellectuals, spiced with vodka and ideas. This was part of the magic of time travel. Denis Hills, in the 1930s, time-travelled to a world of cavalry officers in gleaming boots, of peasants and drunks and urban villains of a kind that had not been seen in England since the days of Dickens. Later, in the '50s and '60s, it was the ladies in hats and gloves, the ice-cream made from real cream, the smell of real bread, students in suits and ties for exams, women holding hands in the streets, café society. It was the place of etiquette in social intercourse, with hand shaking and kissing; the role of the family and relationships between children and parents. For Jessica Munns, it was travelling into the set for *Murder on the Orient Express*, and further back, 'into a Breughel landscape'. Sean Molloy in 1980s Kraków was reminded of 'Attlee's and Churchill's Britain' by the thick fogs, as well as the 'troops of smokers and the military policemen prowling in threes, sniffing out AWOL national servicemen'. All this built up for the lecturers a magic world with which they had a special relationship. 'Why do you persist in treating Poland as a normal country?' one of the authors in this volume wrote to me recently. And it was not, of course, a normal country for the Poles, either: they were the chosen people, in bondage in Egypt.

Some aspects of time-frozen, transmural society appeared more and more outlandish as the 1960s wore into the '70s and the '80s. Polish attitudes to race and class often brought the British lecturers up short. Attitudes to social class came out, for example, in their Polish colleagues' opposition to the system of 'points' for social origin in university entrance exams, a forerunner of positive discrimination which was widely criticised in the 1960s by the Polish intelligentsia. And perhaps above all, there was the question of Polish attitudes to the Jews, which comes up again and again in these lecturers' accounts. By the 1980s, Polish approaches to questions of gender were added to the list of ideological solecisms that came in for horrified criticism.

I am afraid that I cannot pass over these issues without a little uncomfortable moralising. If you travel in time and space, you can't expect to feel entirely at home. The lecturers came to Poland in a period of open class war. For the average member of the Polish intelligentsia, the peasant and worker had until recently represented an impenetrable estate, whose manners and mores were quite as unintelligible as those of the Zulus to the

Emma Harris

19th century British. Just as the Hottentot Venus attracted crowds when she was paraded in London, so the Polish intelligentsia took an interest in any specimens of this strange breed that found their way into town. The post-War revolution had moreover – in a pattern that never operated in Britain (until the very end of the 20th century, when positive discrimination seems to have arrived with a bang) – suddenly placed persons of this kind in authority over the middle classes. The harking on ancestry, gentry status, and breeding in general, was part of nostalgia for what had been lost, and of an impotent fury at being on the losing side.

The willingness of Poles to talk about who was or was not a Jew, both at home and abroad, was something even more disturbing for the British of the '50s and '60s generation. They came to Poland when – in the aftermath of the War – such open categorisations would have been anathema in Britain, although, incidentally, mention of ethnic Jewish origins seems to be OK again in the United Kingdom from the 1980s, if the British press is anything to go by. I do not wish to appear here as an apologist for the strong current of anti-Semitism which undoubtedly has existed in post-War Polish life, but I would again urge the readers of this volume to remember that Polish and British experiences in this area were quite different. Immediately post-War Poland had a strong memory of the community of Orthodox Jews who did not speak their language, dressed differently and were strange and exotic in their habits and observances. I am not talking here about memory of the Jewish middle class who had contributed so much to Polish public life and culture, but about a foreign people and culture from whom the educated Jews also felt alienated – a pattern which is confirmed in many ghetto memoirs, when the two groups found themselves lumped together by the Nazis. It was entirely natural, indeed inevitable, in pre-War Poland to notice whether or not someone was a Jew. Denis Hills does it, too: looking out of his window in ulica Hoża, he saw 'Jews – some in long gabardine coats and high boots wearing fur-lined hats'. It was as though in late 20th century Twickenham, he looked out of his window and saw Pakistani women in saris – or Scotsmen in kilts, come to that.

This visible division of society lingered on in the folk

and family memory of the post-War period. Meanwhile, recalling what had been and had passed was reinforced by Communist pietism about the Holocaust. It is this fading but clear-cut past that was being re-sought in the desire for definition. I am not claiming that there was a neutrality of attitude between the two communities, but that a certain percentage of the interest was ethnographic and neutral. Jewish friends of mine in Poland are also interested in defining who is descended from this lost group. Hostility was there before the War – just as it was in Britain – and it was allegedly reinforced in the 1950s by the presence of Jews in the Communist hierarchy and apparatus. As the Jews themselves disappeared, 'Jewish' increasingly became a term applied to people and institutions of which one disapproved, rather than disapproving of people or institutions because they were Jewish. By the 1960s at least, young people had no real personal experience of a Jewish community of the pre-War kind; later on, after the purges of 1968, they had little experience of Jews of any kind. But the concept continued to circulate: if something was wrong, then it was called Jewish (in somewhat the same way as the verb 'to jew' was current in dialect English certainly into the 1960s or '70s; I would like to add here the verb 'to welsh', but the Oxford Dictionary of English Etymology tells me that the origin of this is unknown). 'Jew' was a political term of abuse, wheeled out by the right wing, perhaps in somewhat the same way that 'Catholic' was used in 18th and early 19th century England: a term of abuse the use of which by the 1990s divided right from left in Polish politics.

Later, for the feminists, Polish attitudes to gender took on similar colours. In a way, these questions were disguised until 1980, when suddenly Solidarity posters in the buses urged women to get back into the home and family. This was a real surprise. For a British student in the '60s, it had been a revelation to find that there had been, for example, respected female economists in Poland in the early part of the 20th century; that a large number of senior university professors were female; that most dentists and a large number of doctors and judges were women. One wondered where all the men were (the answer, of course, as everywhere else in the world, was: in better-paid jobs). But women were confident and outspoken in a way that British

Emma Harris

women learnt only in the last two decades of the century, Poland being, of course, a matriarchal society in which the men drank and the women worked. The sex war had been going on throughout, in far more lethal forms than the West currently dreamed of. Therefore much of the imported feminism of the '80s seemed faked. I knew a (female) Council lecturer in that period (not in literature, this time, but applied linguistics), who came to see me, white with horror, after a Polish lesson. She had discovered that the Polish language used different verb and adjective forms for men and women – and that mixed groups of men and women took the male form. 'Something will have to be done about it', she said. Gender issues of this kind tailed in the 1990s into similar righteous horror about Polish attitudes to homosexuality. None of the writers in this volume has raised the question, but it was one that exercised a number of literature lecturers over the last decade of the century. Most of them, again, wished to find in Poland a replica of the society that they had left. Their indignation about Polish performance on these shibboleths somehow seems to have been heightened by the fact that the Poles were white and European: they couldn't allow for cultural differences within that framework.

Some of the lecturers got stuck at this point. Foreigners were funny: they had the wrong attitudes; they threw British Council lecturers to the floor for sex before confession on All Souls' Eve; they talked openly and abusively about topics which were banned in polite Western society; they adored the Polish Pope. In other words, the love affair became a tug-of-war – the purchase of a mail-order Eastern bride who unexpectedly proved to have a mind of her own. Against this background there was always present – a point which is not much dwelt on in these essays – the subtly insidious relationships that grow up between those who have money and those who don't. In this, as I have said, the Council lecturers were unprecedentedly on the moneyed side of the bargain. Although many of the lecturers cried poor – to the quite justified fury, in absolute terms of comparison, of their Polish colleagues – the cash provided by their Council subsidy certainly gilded the lily. This had charm for both sides: the lecturers could dine daily like lords in quaintly old-fashioned restaurants, and generously entertain their colleagues; the colleagues could enjoy the thrill of Johnny Walker and Seagrams, and other luxuries with a decadent Western taint. In the end, tinges of resentment could be detected on both sides.

For the latecomers of the '90s (not much represented in this sample, apart from recidivists) the charm did not work so well. Some of the lecturers now came from materially under-privileged circumstances themselves: unemployed Ph.D.s, the products of the new mass-production higher education circuit in the U.K., used to living on a pittance in unattractive accom-modation. Some were early-retired refugees from the rat race of the British universities. The conditions of the Polish academic did not always seem to them so very frightful, and the situation of the universities not so very different from what they had left behind. Their pill was still sugared by the Council's salary sup-plement, but this no longer made them lords of the earth. Their Polish colleagues, admittedly often by dint of long hours of scurrying between places of employment, were able to outdo them in income and consumer spending. Hence they had no time to spend with the lecturers long nights of the soul, and their inclination to do so was anyway reduced by their increased access to the realities of Western society. The old magic ceased at long last to work. Curiously, at the same time, with the emer-gence of ideological fashions in the British universities of the 1980s and 1990s, there was perhaps among young Polish aca-demics a greater tendency to treat the lecturers as intellectual gurus than had existed before. Instead of bringing to Poland the trappings of an absolutely foreign world, they brought the fashionable mouthings of the centre to the peripheries.

It is surprising, with hindsight, how little politics entered the relationship at least until the 1980s – politics of the formal or Cold War kind. Most of the lecturers held views very much to the 'left' of the Polish academics and students they encountered, but somehow this didn't matter very much, was hardly noticed, until Solidarity emerged. There were a few politico-historical red herrings that surprised the lecturers: that Churchill was regarded as someone who had betrayed Poland at Yalta; that Lloyd George still had a bad press for his stance at the Paris Peace Conference on the question of Poland's borders; that – going even further back – Napoleon was seen as a hero, fighting for liberty. The Poles were surprised by resolute flaunting of working class origins, ignorance of the *Almanac de Gotha* and anti-Americanism. Communism and the current political system lay somewhere in the background and hardly came into the relationship. The Polish universities by the 1960s were in many ways highly liberal, and took little interest in what the Council lecturers might have been telling their students (this despite occasional glimpses of paranoia in these pieces). The British perhaps take naturally to being agin the government, and accepted the ubiquitous Polish version of this attitude as a matter of course. And so it was only when Polish convictions about life in society crept out of the woodwork, and began to be voiced more loudly after the movement of 1980, that encounters on this plane emerged. Many lecturers and ex-lecturers were disillusioned by how right wing their friends had 'become'.

What do the lecturers' accounts leave out? I have remarked on how little they note about the nature of the institutions by which they were employed – in other words, the Polish universities. They concentrate on details: for example, the educational advantages of their own close-reading approach over the encyclopaedic/theoretical approach favoured by host departments. There is quite a lot of direct or implied criticism in this, a tinge of superiority, more than a touch of neo-colonialism. They tagged along their own intellectual baggage, seeking the fulfilment of the individual and failing to appreciate that the Polish universities, within their own frame of reference, were seeking the greater good of the greatest number. The lecturers by and large failed to see the determined struggle that was going on around them throughout this time, and which continues, to protect the academic freedom of the universities, ensure their institutional continuity and maintain their status and prestige. If they had noticed, there might have been something they could have learned: they might perhaps have developed strategies to combat the undermining of the structures of British higher education in the late 20th century, to which Michael Irwin and George Hyde refer.

Nor do the lecturers take much interest – as far as we can tell from these pieces – in the academic work of their colleagues. The students (products of course of this dull and implicitly criticised system), by contrast, are almost invariably praised for high intelligence and flair. Through contact with Council lecturers, students undoubtedly had their eyes opened to new possibilities and styles. They also acquired techniques of familiar and superficially equal communication with academic staff which were as yet unknown at Polish universities – and sometimes used them in manipulative games against the established hierarchy. It seems with hindsight that the pattern of lecturers' relationships with students was often highly – if unconsciously – manipulative. Students in Poland represented a key not only to lost youth, but also to the magical and inaccessible culture on the other side of the classroom door. For Polish students, the lecturers represented a new power source which, because lost in their world, could be used for immediate advantage and possibly longer-term gain.

So – what did the Polish departments of English make of it all? What did the lecturers look like from the other side of the fence? For Polish colleagues, too, it was easy to stop at the point of superficial encounter. Dirty shoes (why in the '60s did the English stop cleaning their shoes?), unpressed clothes, foul domestic circumstances, encouraging their children (if there were any) to do as they liked, social informality or familiarity, colonial attitudes ('Have you heard of Proust?': one of my distinguished colleagues, a professor of the Catholic University of Lublin, swears that he was asked by a Council lecturer in the 1980s). All this was material for anecdotes and contributed to what amounted almost to a new stereotype of the Englishman – not quite as bad as the American, who would put his feet on the table in the seminar room, but bad enough. It is not surprising that sometimes Polish departments of English wanted to revert to an outdated stereotype: we would like an emeritus professor from an ancient university, one department told the Council in the 1980s, when a candidate was being recruited for a BC job.

Despite occasional anecdotal gaucheness, the Council lecturers received a great deal of attention. Polish scholars and students of English were entranced – especially in the early period, when foreign travel was very restricted – to find happening in the flesh that of which they had read and heard. They were also entranced when the unexpected happened: when the British

Council sent someone non-stereotypical. And the lecturers were overwhelmed by the amount of personal attention they received in this context, and translated it as 'sexiness'. In the end, as with so much of the workings of higher education, it all came down to the impact of individuals. Individuals did a good job, the same kind of good job that anyone can do anywhere. They brought the new ideas and sparkings that any new individual brings to any university department. As for cultural diplomacy, who knows?

One thing, however, is indisputable: that many of the lecturers went on to become cultural diplomats for the Polish cause. They could not bear to sever their links with Poland after their term of employment was over. Michael Irwin refers to the twinge of loss that he felt when crossing the Polish border; he came back again and again, and has retained much-valued links with the Kraków English Department. Denis Hills, half a century after crossing the Polish border for Roumania in 1939 felt compelled to come back to see Poland again, writing about his experiences in *Return to Poland*. Some of the lecturers, notably George Hyde, became translators and champions of Polish literature and drama. This was perhaps not quite what the British Council intended, but it was without doubt a valuable contribution to European integration and understanding.

---

[1]   *A Bird in the Bush*, London, 1936.

Note on the Contributors

Peter J. Conradi was Council lecturer in Kraków (1990-92). Emeritus Professor of English at the University of Kingston, he is currently at work on a biography of Iris Murdoch.

Stoddard Martin was Council lecturer in Łódź (1990-91) and Warsaw (1991-92). He has written widely on Romanticism and Modernism and retains a visiting lectureship at the University of Warsaw.

Alastair Niven was for a decade Director of Literature at the Arts Council of Great Britain. Since 1997 he has held the same position for the British Council.

Denis Hills taught English in Warsaw before the War and married the daughter of one of Poland's most notable writers of Jewish descent (Leśmian). He published accounts of his years in Poland in *Return to Poland* (1988), *Tyrants and Mountains* (1992) and in *The Spectator* and *London Magazine*. Other experiences in his long and colourful career include being imprisoned and sentenced to death in 1975 by Idi Amin.

Witold Ostrowski was in 1938 one of the first Polish scholars to be awarded a Council grant to study in England. After the War he went on to lecture in English at the University of Łódź and to become its longest-serving Head of Department.

Frank Tuohy was the first Council lecturer in Kraków (1958-61). Novelist and biographer of Yeats, his *The Ice-Saints* and short stories set in Poland remain classic accounts of the early post-Stalinist period.

Derwent May was the first Council lecturer in Łódź (1959-63); there he married one of his best students. For many years he was editor of *The Listener*. Currently he writes for *The Times*.

Michael Irwin was Council lecturer in Lublin (1958-59) and

Łódź (1963-64) following Derwent May. He is now Professor of English Literature at the University of Kent at Canterbury.

Sean Molloy was Council lecturer in Kraków (1983-87) and Lublin (1988-93). Having taught in several other corners of the world, he is now retired and lives with his wife in rural Yorkshire, where he is at work on a novel about Poland.

Stephen Romer was Council lecturer in Łódź (1990-91). His poetry, published by OUP, includes *Plato's Ladder* (1994) which contains several poems related to his Polish experience. He now lectures at the University of Tours.

George Hyde was Council lecturer in Lublin (1976-79) and Kraków (1992-93). He is a lecturer at the University of East Anglia and translator of Polish into English. During his three years in Lublin he was regularly trailed by the secret police.

Jessica Munns was Council lecturer in Bydgoszcz (1977-79) and Lublin (1979-83). She is now a professor at the University of Denver. She has published widely in her field, Restoration and 18th century literature, her books including a reader in cultural studies and a critical work on the plays of Thomas Otway.

Gary Mead was Council lecturer in Bydgoszcz (1979-83) following Jessica Munns. He has since worked for the BBC, Granada TV and the *Financial Times* and is now editor and head of research at the World Gold Council.

Cathal McCabe was Council lecturer in Łódź (1991-97). He now lives in Warsaw with his Polish wife and two children and is in charge of special literary events at the Council there.

Emma Harris has lived in Poland since 1968. She is director of the English Institute at the University of Warsaw.